Love Notes
on
His Pillow

Love Notes on His Pillow

And Other Everyday Ways
to Keep Your Love Alive

Linda J. Gilden

new
hope
PUBLISHERS

Birmingham, Alabama

New Hope® Publishers
P. O. Box 12065
Birmingham, AL 35202-2065
www.newhopepublishers.com

Library of Congress Cataloging-in-Publication Data

Gilden, Linda Jeffords.
  Love notes on his pillow : and other everyday ways to keep
your love alive / Linda J. Gilden.
      p. cm.
  Includes bibliographical references.
  ISBN 1-59669-014-3 (softcover)
  1. Marriage. 2. Communication in marriage. 3. Love. I.
Title.
  HQ734.G434 2006
  646.7'8--dc22
                                    2005028999

ISBN: 1-59669-014-3

N064137 • 0206 • 8.5M1

Dedication

This book is dedicated to
the biggest love noter of all,
Jesus Christ.
To Him be all the glory.

Table of Contents

Love notes can be handwritten on paper, or they
can also be small gestures, spoken words, or random
surprises that make your spouse feel special.
Discovering and practicing your spouse's special
love language in your love noting will strengthen
your marriage.

Love notes can be the fuel that ignites the fire
of romance, or nuggets of encouragement that
make your spouse feel more secure. Just a few
short words on his pillow or in the briefcase can
make your husband feel truly loved. Practicing
love noting regularly will help the two of you
keep your love alive.

These creative ideas for holidays, birthdays,
and anniversaries will help you plan celebrations
your spouse will never forget.

Many days are special and worthy of extra effort.
Don't miss an opportunity—make every day a day
to say, "I love you."

Acknowledgments

My experience of being showered daily with love notes from my husband, John, led to the writing of this book. Thank you, John, for making me feel like your queen every day. Your expressions of love take many forms, and I am so blessed to be your wife. Our marriage is a precious gift from our loving Heavenly Father.

A lifestyle of love noting comes naturally for me because of the example set by my parents. I am thankful I grew up with a daily view of how to love those around me creatively.

I pray that my children will always experience the joy of finding new ways to say, "I love you." May God bless you, my children, your marriages, and Carson, our granddaughter, who arrived to us with God's handprints all over her. You are all special love notes from God to me.

To Andrea Mullins, Rebecca England, and all the wonderful New Hope staff, thank you for your commitment to excellence. I have appreciated so much your encouragement, support, and shared excitement about the message of *Love Notes on His Pillow*. May your lives be filled with love notes.

To all those who read the manuscript and prayed with and for me during the process of *Love Notes on His Pillow*, thank you. Friends are a treasure and I thank God for each one of you.

To all who shared their stories, thank you. May God add His blessing to every love note.

Introduction

Communication is important to marriage. A good marriage requires talking with each other, listening to each other, understanding each other, and honestly sharing innermost feelings. Time spent communicating is priceless.

Today's society does not always make it easy to communicate with those we love. We want things fast and without a lot of trouble. Our society is full of *instants*: instant coffee, instant messages, fast food, oil changes in a jiffy, and the list goes on. Couples spend less time together than ever before. These days, more families seem to require two incomes, which means both husband and wife are rushing off to work in the morning and returning home tired at night. Jobs that require travel keep families apart for days at a time.

In the midst of busy schedules, couples must find a way to stay close and keep the lines of communication open. They must keep in touch and find out the important things going on in each other's lives before that information becomes old news.

God has actually shown us and left us instructions as to how to do that. In Jeremiah 31:3, He says, "I have loved you with an everlasting love; I have drawn you with loving-kindness."

I believe the last part of that verse could read, "I have drawn you with love notes." God is the Master of love notes. He continually shows us His love in both large and small ways, and He uses every type of love note to do so.

Every day presents many opportunities for us to bless our spouses with love notes: written notes, acts of service, deeds, phone calls, or other actions that say, "I love you, and I want to be part of your life." Receiving a love note makes that person feel special, loved, and valued.

Love noting does not stop with the recipient. Love noting definitely creates a "ripple effect." Our loved one is blessed, and often the lives of those around him are touched as well. When we have children, they observe the love that is exchanged between their parents. Love noting is being modeled to them. They will learn how to be thoughtful communicators by observing how it is done.

I watched my parents write notes to one another and do thoughtful things each day just to make the life of the other a little easier. I prayed that someday I would have someone who would write love notes to me and for whom I could find creative ways of saying "I love you." God sent me what I prayed for, and as my marriage grew, John and I quickly realized the value of an occasional love note. We have also seen our children become third generation note writers.

Effective communication takes practice and requires effort. Love noting can be a big part of that. Begin now by thinking of those whom you love. What would please them? A written note, an unexpected gift, an act of service, a short visit? Begin to be intentional in showing those around you how much you care. You will not only notice a ripple effect, but also a boomerang effect. The love you express to others will be multiplied as it comes back to you.

Chapter One

What Is a Love Note?

I slowly walked into my office. Last night had been a late night of writing and I was still a little weary. As I plopped into my chair, I looked to the right of my computer. There was a fresh Diet Coke—a fountain drink, not a can—my favorite treat, with a straw perched on top. "I love you" was the message written in permanent marker on the top of the lid. My husband knew I needed a little encouragement with my upcoming deadline. He may not be able to write for me, but he surely knows how to be my head cheerleader. I smiled that day as I took the paper off the straw. I took a long sip of my drink. Many days when I catch a glimpse of that empty cup with the love note on the lid sitting on my shelf, it brings a smile to my face and a warm feeling to my heart.

You may think this book is only about written love notes. True, we will address those and provide lots of creative ideas for written notes. However, the term *love note* actually refers to much more—it refers to any outward expression that offers encouragement, love, or pleasure to the recipient.

Gary Chapman, author of *The Five Love Languages*, suggests that all individuals have a love language, a method of expressing love that speaks loudest to them. Those languages are (1) acts of service, (2) quality time, (3) words of affirmation, (4) physical touch, (5) and gifts. Chapman says that unless you express love to your spouse in his or her love language, he or she won't understand the message. In essence, you are speaking entirely different languages.

Many times, a love note will be the traditional piece of paper with a hastily jotted sentiment. Other times, it may be a piece of favorite candy strategically hidden, a forgotten stack of laundry lovingly folded, or a glass of water delivered to a thirsty but too-busy-to-stop writer.

Throughout my life, I have collected many love notes from my husband and other members of my family. The outward expression may be different, but the sentiment is always the same: I love you!

Since the development of the sticky notes, notes can be penned and attached in just a matter of a few minutes. Stick them everywhere: in his car, on her favorite chair, in the briefcase, and even in the shower. If you are going to put one in the shower, however, enclose it in a plastic bag so the ink won't run!

I learned to leave love notes for my loved ones from observing my parents. My mother often took my sister and me along with her on antiquing trips. She loved to go to New England or London in search of a few small treasures. I remember Mom's delight when, as we arrived at the hotel and unpacked our bags, she discovered small scraps of paper bearing a message in my father's familiar handwriting sprinkled throughout her suitcase. Mom found them folded inside her underwear, stuffed into her shoes, and tucked in her coat pocket or change purse.

"Susie" (that was Dad's pet name for Mom), they would often begin, "I hope you and the girls have fun. I will miss you. Hurry home to me."

After returning home, Mom unpacked her antique treasures and added them to her collection. The next things she unpacked were her notes, carefully smoothing and refolding them to put away for safekeeping. She put them in the bottom drawer of an antique spice rack that hung over the vanity in her bathroom.

Not until she died did I realize how many notes Mom had saved. When I tried to open the bottom drawer, it was so stuffed with love notes I could hardly open it. Seeing so many precious notes made me decide that my own notes needed a place for safekeeping. We carefully packed Mama's notes away and cleaned out the drawer.

When we finished cleaning out Mom's house, I took that spice rack to hang in my own home on the wall in my bathroom. I immediately began to save my love notes in the bottom drawer. It isn't yet full, but I add to my collection frequently.

A love note may seem like a little thing. It's not the size that makes a difference—it's the expression of love that creates an effect. The effects of a few words or a small deed can be monumental.

My parents knew the value of love notes. I'm thankful that my husband and I have followed their example and discovered for ourselves the joy of saying "I love you" in simple, creative ways.

We live in a world that moves at a pretty hectic pace. Everyone works long days and is in a hurry: a quick kiss and we're out the door into separate cars to different destinations; an instant message on the computer and we have made plans for the day. Yet even one or two words can stick with us throughout the day, and their meaning can speak volumes.

*L*ove Notes Can Be . . .

. . . WRITTEN ON PAPER

The word *note* usually brings to mind a piece of paper with a message written on it. This is the traditional love note. The wonderful thing about a written love note is that it can be saved and read again and again. The recipient can experience the original joy and encouragement many times. This way of showing love is a classic for a good reason, and can be enjoyed by both men and women.

Words can mean so much, especially when they come from someone who loves us. They have the power to bless, encourage, uplift, and turn an otherwise cloudy day into one full of sunshine. Just a few words from someone who loves us can give us the courage to face a busy day, make a difficult business presentation, or meet the needs of three energetic toddlers. Because words can also be misunderstood and unintentionally hurt the recipient, we need to choose them carefully.

Never put anything in writing that is not positive. Negative words will be remembered long after a conversation is finished. I have heard that it takes many positive comments to undo the damage of just one negative one, so be positive with your spouse whenever possible.

If you spend your days at a computer, sending your love notes by email is certainly acceptable. Let the recipient transfer them to paper, or, if preferable, he can make a special file in the computer and pull them up to reread whenever encouragement is needed.

. . . STUCK ON SOMETHING

Stickers and sticky notes are a quick and easy way to say "I love you." Many varieties are available in stores today. Some are printed with the words *I love you*. Others convey a subtle message. For example, perhaps you have just spent a wonderful getaway weekend at the beach. A few beach stickers strategically placed during the weeks after returning home will remind your spouse of the sweet memories. A sticker representing a special interest of your spouse, such as golf, tennis, or reading, also says, "I know you and love you." Knowing your spouse's special interests and finding ways to acknowledge those interests provide unique opportunities for expressing your love.

. . . A SEEMINGLY RANDOM ACT

An act or chore done spontaneously doesn't go unnoticed by your spouse. Stop by the sink to wash dirty dishes, gather the garbage on trash day so it's ready to go to the curb, make sure the sheets are straight when you get into the bed. Our bedtime ritual includes making sure the princess doesn't have to sleep on the pea. (Our mattress pad refuses to stay straight under the sheets. Knowing that, my husband reaches under the sheet to make sure the pad and sheets are straight before I come to bed, and I don't have to sleep on a bump!)

Recently, while in the middle of a project, I hurriedly served supper and then rushed back to the computer so as not to lose my train of thought.

"Excuse me," I said, leaving the table. "I'll come back, put the food up, and do the dishes in a little while."

Three hours later, I realized I had not followed through on this. I jumped up from the computer and went to the kitchen. Imagine my delight when I walked into a spotless kitchen. The food was in the refrigerator, dishes were in the dishwasher, and countertops were shining.

The effectiveness of this type of love note is the element of surprise. Such acts speak loudly because your spouse doesn't expect them. The surprise element makes this type of love note special. If an act becomes routine, it may lose its effectiveness.

. . . A Specially Planned Outing

Dates don't have to stop when you get married. In fact, it's not a bad idea to step up your dating habits. Many couples think that means spending lots of money, but dates don't have to be expensive. Even trips to the grocery store can be fun when you do it together.

Take turns with your spouse planning a night out. Whoever makes the plan for the evening must choose something he or she thinks will be fun for the spouse. Keep in mind common interests. Make it a goal to spend as little money as possible so you don't feel guilty about the cost of the evening.

Some great options for love notes of time are:

♥ **Have a picnic outdoors.** This could be as simple as fixing your dinner plates and sitting on the porch to eat or as elaborate as actually preparing a picnic complete with fried chicken and red checkered tablecloth.

If the weather doesn't permit an outdoor picnic, why not plan a fast food picnic? Arrange ahead of time to eat at your favorite fast food restaurant. Pack a basket with tablecloth, real plates and glasses, flatware, and of course, a candle. When you get to the restaurant, order your food. While you are waiting for your order, spread the tablecloth on a table in one corner of the restaurant, and prepare the table. When you get your food, transfer it from the paper wrappers and cups to your plates and glasses. Enjoy your fancy fast food picnic!

♥ **Pretend you are tourists in your hometown.** Visit the ballpark, the museum, the library, parks, and other places of interest.

♥ **Play inside games.** Board games and cards provide fun activities during which conversation can happen. If your husband is a video game buff, play video games with him, and let him win!

♥ **Take a drive.** If you both like to look at houses, ride around and explore the home construction in your area. If you like water, drive to a lake and enjoy the sunset.

♥ **Invite your mate to a special dinner.** Create a formal invitation to a special surprise dinner, and mail it to your mate. Go to a favorite restaurant and share a meal.

♥ **Read a book together.** This can be done different ways: (1) You can both read the same book and be prepared to discuss it when you have time together. That sounds a little like high school, but you will be surprised at the rabbit trails your discussions will take! (2) If you prefer, you can read the book together—literally. Choose a topic you will both enjoy, and read a chapter at a time when you are together. This will take a little longer, but you will be enjoying the book at the same pace. Make it a date night. Have dinner or coffee at a local café and spend an extra hour reading to one another.

. . . A Purposely Chosen Gift

You may want to put gifts in a separate category from love notes and call them *love gifts*. However, an item especially chosen for your spouse can be a loud declaration of love. For our purpose we will talk about love gifts as love notes.

Pick a single flower from the rose garden on your way into the house. If you don't have a flower garden, plan next spring to make a small cutting garden near your house. It will be easy for you to pick a flower for your spouse as you enter the house.

I love folded potato chips. When my husband and I eat potato chips together, he just smiles and, without saying a word, hands over the folded chips from his bag to me as he comes to them. Each one of those is a love note to me.

As a writer, I love pens. When a salesman at work gives my husband a new pen, it often becomes a gift to me.

One week my husband was very busy. Usually home for supper, this particular week he was lucky to get home by bedtime. I knew the state of our yard was bothering him, especially the height of the grass. I don't do much yard work, and I knew I couldn't take care of this for him, so I hired the teenager across the street to come over and cut the grass. John was amazed that I even thought about doing that. It took one big thing off his mind during his busy week.

With love gifts, the cost is not the important issue. The gesture that results from a spouse's thoughtfulness is worth more than a monetary value.

. . . A SIMPLE HUG OR TOUCH

You know better than anyone else the special touch that means the most to your spouse.

Often when we hold hands, my husband will squeeze mine three times. That means, "I love you." When I squeeze back four times, that means, "I love you, too" or "I love you more." The conversation may continue: "I love you much more" or "I love you so very much." It becomes a game, and eventually we get all mixed up and dissolve in laughter.

. . . SPEAKING YOUR SPOUSE'S NAME

Sometimes just to hear the one you love say your name is a treat. My husband says my name in a way that no one else does. Just to hear him say it warms my heart and often makes me want to giggle in delight.

We have always used our real names but many couples have pet names. Asbury and Mildred used to call one another "Sweet Thing." However, over the years it evolved into "Fee Fang" and became their special name for each other. Once the names were established, Asbury began to sign his notes "FF," and Mildred signed her notes

"½ ff." Their Christmas present tags read "To: FF, Love, ½ ff" or "To: ½ ff, I Love You, FF."

As newlyweds, we lived far away from home and attended a small church where we knew very few people. The first time we met the pastor, he said, "I want you to meet my wife." Turning to a pretty lady nearby, he said, "Wiffie, come here a minute please. I have some folks I want you to meet."

I had never heard anyone by that name, but I soon learned that his wife's first name was not Wiffie. Wiffie was a nickname he had devised from the word *wife* as a special term of endearment for his wife. She, in turn, called him "Hub."

One of the sweetest ways to hear your spouse speak your name is in prayer. It is a great blessing to hear your spouse thank God for you. In Sam's prayer before the meal, he often thanks God for his wife, Ginger. "When Sam first did that years ago," says Ginger, "I felt self-conscious. I thought he needed to keep the attention on God, not mentioning me. But through the years, I have grown to accept these 'eavesdropping' compliments and appreciate a loving husband who brings me before God."

. . . AN ACROSTIC OR POEM

An acrostic is a creative way to send a special message of love. As a means of encouragement, make an acrostic using each letter in your spouse's name to list some of his or her finer characteristics. Have a great time with it! Wax poetic if you can. A list of possible affirmative words is in the Appendix. A few examples follow.

D elightful   **M** arvelous
A wesome   **A** dorable
V ibrant   **R** avishing
I rresistible   **Y** outhful
D ashing

You may want to personalize even more. Write a poem using the letters of your spouse's name as the first letter of each line. Make it as silly or serious as you like.

J ust walking around the yard one day,
O utside the leaves all seemed to say,
H e's the one, the best for you;
N o one else will ever do!

H eaven and earth will never find
A nyone so sweet or cute or kind.
N ever has there been a girl,
N ever in the whole wide world,
A s perfect as you are for me.
H ow thankful I will always be.

Unlimited Options

"I've found almost anything can be a love note," my friend Lissa says. "Sharing tasks that are usually his. Asking him to tell me about his mountaineering adventures. Being proud of him in front of others. Running errands for him. Cutting out articles I think he'd like." All of those are love notes when you do them for your spouse.

Love notes come in many forms, shapes, and sizes, but the most important thing about a love note is the heartfelt message.

Chapter Two

Love Notes
Make a Difference

Think about it. When someone compliments us, it makes us feel good. When someone appreciates us, we feel that we have value. When someone takes the time to notice we are having a hard day and reaches out to hug us, we feel like God Himself has wrapped His arms around us. Whether we are in the workplace, at church, or in the midst of day-to-day parenting, a small note or token of someone's affection can be a tremendous encouragement. It can change our perspective on the day and make us smile.

On days when we feel like we just can't keep up the pace, encouragement prevents us from giving up. On days when the sun is shining and everything seems right with the world, encouragement affirms that feeling. On days when we feel like no one loves us or cares anything about what is happening in our lives, just a few words of encouragement can change our perspective.

I'm not much of a sports fan, but I have been to enough soccer games, swim meets, and other events to know that encouragement makes a difference. Have you ever been to a race and watched the faces of the runners? Most of them don't look like they are having a lot of fun. Yet when they pass a group of people in the crowd who are cheering for *them*, their countenance changes. They *can* go on. They can *do it.* They receive a sudden burst of energy from those who believe in them. Encouragement makes a difference. No matter what the task at hand, a little encouragement goes a long way.

Because I grew up in a family of note writers, I have a collection of notes saved over the years. Some of them are just a few words on now-yellowed paper. One of them still resides in the pocketbook I took on my honeymoon. It is from my dad. I also have the first note my husband wrote to me over 35 years ago. That one is simply on a small piece of composition book paper. It stirs my heart every time I see that familiar handwriting and remember how long it has been! I also have more recent notes, such as the one I carry in my briefcase (it was written by my then six-year-old son) and the one taped to my mirror several short years ago. No matter how old they are, every time I read them, I feel blessed again; I feel special, I feel important, I feel loved.

Validation and encouragement are important to us wherever we are. The place that it means the most is at home in our marriages. A few well-chosen words from our mates go a long way.

In their book, *The Love List,* Drs. Les and Leslie Parrott explain that "a few small actions—practiced on a daily, weekly, monthly, and yearly basis—can change everything for a couple. Little deliberate behaviors quietly lavish love on a marriage."

When your spouse is having a hard week at work or at home, a little extra time spent encouraging him or her will make a big difference. That quietly lavished love will strengthen your marriage while adding humor and spontaneity to each day.

Strategically Placed Notes

Sara knew her husband, Greg, was preparing for a big presentation at work toward the end of the week. She wanted to leave him alone so he could focus on his work, but she wanted him to know how much she loved him and believed in him.

Every night that week when Greg went to bed, he found a note on his pillow. Each one was handwritten and sealed in an envelope. The first one said, "Thank you for working so hard for your family. We really appreciate it." The second night's note read, "I would accept any project you presented. I love you." On the third night, the note to Greg said, "This presentation is going to give you the opportunity to really shine. And you'll see me shining, too, because I am so proud of you."

By presentation time, Greg had so much self-confidence he couldn't wait to get to the boardroom and sell his idea to those present.

In her family, Jane is the one who travels in her business. On one occasion, she wanted to make sure Larry didn't miss her love note when he went to bed alone.

She pulled a solid-colored pillowcase out of the linen closet and spread it out carefully on the kitchen table.

Using permanent markers, she began to draw hearts and red lips and write short messages of love. When she was finished, she had a beautiful work of art and *heart*, brightly colored and filled with love.

Jane went back to the bedroom and switched pillowcases on Larry's pillow. Pulling up the bedspread, she smiled. She could just see Larry's face when he pulled back the cover to crawl into bed that night.

Grabbing her suitcase, she was out the door, knowing her presence would be felt that night even though she would be many miles away.

Hide and Seek Notes

Kristi doesn't travel a lot, but when she does, she tries to make sure Jim feels her love even in her absence. The first time she was gone, she left notes everywhere: in the closet, in his socks, in the bathroom, by the computer, and in the dog food, as well as many other places. Some were left out in the open, and some were hidden inside other things. She tried to think of all the places Jim would be looking for things during the few days she would be gone.

When Kristi called Jim one night, the first thing he wanted to talk about was "all the notes."

"Oh," said Kristi. "Did you find them all?"

"I don't know," Jim answered. "How many did you write?"

The line was silent for a few seconds. "I'm not sure. I didn't count them," she said. He could *hear* the sheepish grin on her face.

For several weeks after that, Kristi or Jim continued to find orphan notes, left with good intentions, but not found by Jim at the intended time. The message was still the same and was received with just as much enthusiasm.

The next time Kristi was going to be away, she did the same thing for Jim. Only this time when he found the first note, he noticed a "1" printed in the corner. Every subsequent note he found had a number on it, and even though he didn't find them in consecutive order, they both knew in the end whether he had retrieved all the notes.

Love note for the dresser drawer: Thanks for doing the laundry. I appreciate having clean clothes to wear.

Love note for the freezer: Wow! It's cold in here, but my heart is warm every time I think of you.

Love note for the lunch box: Thank you for working hard to support our family. We love you.

Love note in the diaper stacker: You are a wonderful parent. Thank you for loving our children.

Love note in the pajama drawer: I will miss sleeping by your side tonight. I can't wait to get home.

Love note in his medicine cabinet: Please stay healthy for us. We need you and love you.

Love note in the refrigerator: Enjoy your snack. I'd like to nibble on you!

Love note on the remote control: You really know how to push the right buttons with me!

I Can Do It

I didn't know I married a farmer. This city girl had no clue how to do anything more than water a houseplant, and she wasn't even very good at that.

When John first said he wanted to plant a garden, he was met with a blank stare.

"Okay," I finally said, "but I don't know a thing about gardening or growing things. I probably won't be able to help you much."

I was pretty good at eating my dad's summer tomatoes, but that was about as close as I got to any kind of farming.

John proceeded to plant a beautiful garden. What he didn't know how to do, he read about and quickly learned. Soon we had many healthy green sprouts throughout the garden in the side yard. People driving by even stopped to admire John's gardening success.

John loved his new hobby so much that he didn't know when to stop. He'd plow for hours without taking a break. Worried that he might have a heat stroke, I frequently took large glasses of water to him. I guess you could call me the farmer's water girl. At that time, it was the only love note I could think of that had to do with the garden. I had seen pictures of women in their straw hats alongside their husbands in the gardens, but I didn't think I fit that profile.

When John picked his first basketful of beans, he came in the house beaming.

"Wow," I said. "What are we going to do with so many beans?"

"Can them, of course," he said.

"Can them?" I replied.

"That's what Mama always did. We couldn't possibly eat this many beans, could we?"

"No, you're right. We couldn't possibly eat them all."

But can beans? I didn't know that was part of this gardening thing. My mother never canned. I thought the only canned beans that existed were those on the vegetable aisle of the grocery store.

I had a friend who had grown up in the country, so I called her.

"Kathy," I said. "I need help."

"What's wrong?" she asked with concern.

"John thinks I am going to can all these beans he has grown. I don't have a clue how to do that. Do you know how to can beans?"

"I sure do. It's really not hard. Want me to come over and show you?"

"Yes, please." I couldn't believe I had discovered a canning angel on my first try!

I went to the store to buy a canner and carefully followed Kathy's instructions on what kind to buy and where to find the right jars and lids. I had never seen such a big pot! By the time I got home, I was convinced home-canned beans were definitely a lot more trouble than the canned beans at the grocery store.

Kathy came over, and we started the bean-canning lesson. I learned how to wash, properly break, and pack the beans. Then came the real canning part: I filled the canner with water, placed the jars in it, sealed it, turned on the stove eye, and watched as the pressure began to rise. Kathy stood beside me to make sure I did nothing wrong. I remember thinking that giant shivering silver pot could take off any minute! However, in just a short amount of time, the buzzer sounded, and it was time to check our handiwork. When the pot was cool enough for us to take off the lid, we saw seven perfectly canned quarts of beans. That wasn't really so hard.

Over the years, I have canned beets, squash, tomatoes and okra, beans, and more beans. Now when the beans are ready for harvest, I get pretty excited about taking out my canner and gathering all the empty jars to get ready for canning!

Canning beans is a *definite* love note at our house. The look on the farmer's face when he admires those canned beans makes it well worth the effort.

Some husbands are not farmers but need help in other ways. Will is color-blind. For as long as they have been married, Elizabeth has picked out Will's clothes for him so his shirts and ties would match. Through the years, they have streamlined the process. Elizabeth now hangs Will's clothes in the closet according to what goes together, so Will can be confident that when he picks out his clothes every day, he will be selecting compatible colors. As for the sock issue, Elizabeth buys only black socks, eliminating the need for Will to match socks with other clothing items every morning.

Elizabeth's help with clothing has been a true love note to Will every day of their marriage. He doesn't have to worry about the embarrassment of arriving at work or at church with mismatched clothing.

Attitude Adjustment

In the book *Love Extravagantly*, Marita Littauer and Chuck Noon share a time when Marita's slight schedule adjustment made a big difference in their marriage. This love note has continued to draw them closer and to keep a spark in every homecoming.

In our marriage, I [Marita] am the one who is often on the road. But Chuck doesn't like that I travel. However, traveling has been a part of my life for all my adult years. When I met Chuck, I was teaching seminars all over the country. I think he should be used to it after 22 years of marriage. Instead, he likes it less and less. Since I do not have the financial freedom to change, and Chuck agrees that my speaking and writing is what God has called me to do, I have had to learn to make adjustments to make my travel schedule work better for our lives.

I am the one who was unhappy with the way things were; I was the one who wanted a change. Coming home on the plane, I often enjoy the relaxing escape of a romance novel. As I read, I picture Chuck meeting me at the gate with roses in his hand. Or at least dropping what he is doing when I walk in the door to hug me, kiss me, and confirm how much he has missed me.

In reality, the plane lands. I walk alone through the terminal, get my baggage, and go to my car. I wait in line to pay for parking and drive home. Because I like to get home from a trip as soon as possible, I frequently arrive late at night rather than the next day. Chuck is often asleep when I get home. I tiptoe in. Drop my bags and undress in the dark. I crawl into bed beside him and he wiggles his toes against my leg to welcome me home. Hardly the romance novel scene I had painted in my mind.

A few years ago, I was scheduled to fly home the day after a seminar, the day of our anniversary. Since it was our anniversary, I really wanted that romance novel scene. The day before I had arranged to have flowers sent to Chuck's office with a card that said "Happy Anniversary! Hurry home!" (I had the flowers delivered in the morning in case he forgot what day it was. They would remind him, and he'd have time to do whatever he needed to do.) I planned to arrive home before he got off work. I had time to shop for the ingredients to make a lovely dinner. I got home, did the dinner prep work, and put it all aside. In the bedroom I found something small and black hanging on our four poster bed with an anniversary card. (He hadn't forgotten after all.) I relaxed in a bubble bath and put my present on. I lit candles in the bedroom and put something bubbly in the silver bucket next to the bed with two crystal flutes. It was nearly time for him to get home. I crawled up on the bed and read my romance novel. I waited. The dogs barked and I heard his car door. I tucked the romance novel away and placed myself artfully across the bed. I could write my own romance novel with the results of my efforts!

Looking back, here is the change I put into play. I had sent Chuck flowers, he knew that I had not forgotten what day it was. He knew I'd be waiting, and he knew what he had waiting for me. He was excited to see me, glad I had come home. While the night left me breathless, I thought it through the next morning. That was the reaction I'd like to get every time I come home!

Romans 12:18 tells me that it is my job to "live at peace with everyone." It does not tell me to change my husband. I thought, *What could I change that would bring about the desired effect?*

First, I could change my schedule so I come home before him, instead of after he was asleep. I could fix a special dinner. I could put on one of the many "little somethings" he has given me over the years, and I can place myself across the bed as if in a lingerie catalog. Yes, I could do that. My next trip I did. It worked again—even without the special day and without the flowers. My next trip I tried it again. It worked again. I had created an attitude adjustment. While he is still not crazy about my traveling, he loves my coming home. Without travel, I wouldn't be putting forth the homecoming effort. (I do not go through my "attitude adjustment" routine every time I come home—it would lose the sense of surprise that makes it special.)

Marvelous Man Notes

Grant and Erin have been married five years. They are enjoying building their life together.

One of the surprises they both discovered when they first got married was that they didn't agree on everything. When they were engaged, people told them that there would be times of disagreement and even a fight or two, but they couldn't imagine that. It didn't take long for Grant and Erin to realize that was true, nor did it take long for them to realize they could creatively work through their disagreements. Sometimes it even became fun.

One day Erin came home from the grocery store. She knew Grant was in the house working on a big project, but she had so many bags and really needed some help unloading the car.

"Grant," she called coming through the door. "Will you come help me unload the groceries?" *It won't take but a few minutes, and he probably needs a break anyway,* she thought.

"I'm really busy, babe."

"Grant, puhleeeeeeeze. I need your help."

"Hang on."

Grant appeared in the doorway of the kitchen. "I'll help on one condition."

"Condition? Oh, come on, Grant. What are you talking about?"

"I'll help you bring in the groceries if you promise to be extra nice to me the rest of the week."

"Grant . . ."

"Those are my terms."

"Oh, all right, just come on. You can just bring them all in. I'll start putting them away."

As she put away the groceries, Erin began formulating a plan of her own. *OK, if he wants extra nice, that's what he is going to get!*

Grant's favorite snack was M&M's. When Erin finished putting things away, she hollered to Grant, "Be back in a minute. I forgot something at the store."

Erin went back to the store and looked down the candy aisle. She bought big packs of M&M's, individual packs, minis, cookies with M&M's, and every little surprise that was remotely related. She even found a notepad, a pencil, and a mug with the logo printed on it.

Back home, Erin fixed a big glass of Grant's favorite sweet iced tea. Quietly entering the office, she put the glass on his coaster and put a pack of M&M's on his stack of papers.

"I love you," she said. "You are my marvelous man. That's what the two M's stand for."

While Grant was working, Erin went into their bedroom. She placed a few packs of the candy in Grant's pajama drawer, his underwear drawer, and his medicine cabinet.

This continued all week as agreed upon. Erin found new places each day to stash the treat to remind Grant that he was her marvelous man. One night before Grant even thought about going to bed, Erin turned back the covers and sprinkled loose candy between the sheets. Then she carefully remade the bed so as not to spoil the surprise.

Usually the late sleeper, Erin got up one morning before Grant and fixed a breakfast tray for him. She served him breakfast in bed: pancakes with a few M&M's sprinkled in them and coffee in his new mug.

Grant was amazed at Erin's creativity.

Long after Erin's week of extra commitment to being nice to Grant was over, she continued to remind him he was her marvelous man. It became her trademark love note.

If he had to leave town on a business trip, she gave his business partner bags of candy to place in his hotel room or to give him before a big presentation. She often left marvelous man surprises in his car, briefcase, or lunch box. When Grant asked Erin to make him a sandwich for lunch, she occasionally slipped one piece of candy in the middle of the sandwich.

Christi and Lee keep a similar exchange going on at their house. Christi loves jelly beans, and they have become a signature item for her. Lee is an exceptional love noter and often leaves written notes for Christi. However, when he doesn't have time to write anything or if he wants to give her a special treat, he leaves a pack of jelly beans.

"A pack of jelly beans is Lee's signature love note," says Christi. "I find them on my pillow, on my computer keyboard, and in the kitchen. Sometimes there is a note and sometimes there is no note. Regardless, I know immediately who was thinking of me and wanted me to feel special. Lee has a way of knowing when I need a pick-me-up of my favorite jelly beans. At the end of an exhausting and challenging day with a toddler, finding a pack of jelly beans warms my heart as a reminder of the love Lee and I share. He knows me so well."

*M*ore Notes to Make a Difference

♥ Purchase or make a small box. Craft and discount stores have them, or you can decorate an empty tissue or gift box. On the outside of the box, write the words, "You are a star." Cut out lots of stars from construction paper. On each star, write one reason why your mate is a star. Reasons could include "You bring me coffee every morning" or "You are the best snuggler." Almost anything will qualify for the status of star. Present this box to him on a special occasion with instructions not to read them all at once.

♥ Address an envelope to your husband or wife and put a blank piece of paper inside. On the outside put his or her name and "Very Important Message." Let your mate open it at a time when you are together. After your mate experiences the shock of seeing a page with nothing on it, give your explanation: "No words can describe how much I love you."

Chapter Three

Celebration Love Notes

Many days are special and worthy of extra effort—worthy of classic love notes being placed on the pillow or in the briefcase. Try some of these creative ideas for making anniversaries, holidays, birthdays, and every day extra special.

Anniversaries

STICKER ANNIVERSARY

For a number of years, our church youth group ski trip took place in the month of February, our anniversary month. Actually, for most of those years, our anniversary date fell during that trip.

Our children were in the youth group, and we liked to go with them on trips whenever possible, so for many years, our anniversary was celebrated with over a hundred young people in a snowy resort! We don't ski anymore, but we really enjoy watching the youth and being around the snow.

One year, a ski trip to West Virginia was planned. We decided to leave a few days early to celebrate our anniversary at a well-known resort near our destination. It was a very fancy place.

When we arrived, we found our room to be elegant; we were greeted with fresh chocolates, a bottle of champagne, complimentary dinner (well, I'm sure it wasn't really complimentary!), and more amenities than you can imagine. Fresh flowers bedecked our room, and a personal note from the manager welcomed us. In the bathroom, our toilet paper was folded neatly and secured with a sticker that bore the seal of the resort.

The toilet paper seal was the most remarkable thing. It seemed as though every time we broke the seal to use the paper, the next time we returned to the bathroom, the toilet paper was again folded nicely and stuck with a new seal. We never saw anyone else enter the bathroom, but mysteriously our paper stayed folded and sealed the entire time we were there.

When our little anniversary retreat ended, we drove over to the ski resort to meet our youth group. This was definitely a switch to the other end of the accommodation scale! I was in a one-bedroom condo with four teenage girls. My husband was in a condo at the other end of the building with four guys. As usual, our young men carried luggage for the ladies and saw to it that we were settled in our rooms.

Once in my room, I went into the bathroom. To my surprise, the toilet paper was folded and stuck with a seal from the resort we had just visited! How in the world did it get there? Thinking it was just a one-time love note,

I removed the sticker and put it in my pocket. It would probably come in handy later.

I went next door, then made my way down the hall to check on others in our group. Everything seemed to be in order. On the way back to my condo, I passed one of the boys staying in my husband's room.

"Ed," I said, "will you do me a favor, please?"

"Sure. Whatcha need?"

Pulling the sticker from my pocket, I said, "See this sticker?"

Ed nodded.

"When you go back to your room, would you go into the bathroom and put this on the toilet paper roll for me? Here, watch." I began to show Ed how to fold the paper before applying the sticker. "Think you can handle that?"

"No problem," Ed replied.

I went back to my condo to call my husband and see how things were going at his end of the building. Chaperones were placed strategically throughout the building; we just ended up staying on opposite ends. Yet, we were able to talk by phone and saw each other on the slopes and at the evening meeting.

A little later, I went into the bathroom. The toilet paper was once again folded neatly and stuck with a sticker! How did he do that?

The saga continued throughout this anniversary ski trip. Every time I went in the bathroom, I saw another *love note* on the toilet paper.

Later I found out my husband had asked the house-keeper at the resort for extra stickers before we left. Many of the youth on the trip had become involved in this endeavor and were very excited to be a part of our unusual anniversary celebration.

No matter where we spend our anniversary, I'm so glad we can stick together!

LOVE NOTE HINT: *Buy a pack of stickers that will remind your spouse of you. If you play tennis, it could be tennis rackets; if he fishes, it could be fish stickers; if you both enjoy music, buy music note stickers. Put stickers in unexpected places (inside his palm pilot case, on the first page of the checkbook, on the toilet paper, etc.) to be discovered by your spouse.*

CANDLELIGHT DINNER FOR 132?

As the lead chaperones on our youth ski trip, we were supposed to be in contact with the 132 persons on the trip at all times through our walkie-talkie radios.

My husband called my room and said, "Would you like to go downstairs to the restaurant for our anniversary dinner?"

"I'd love to," I replied, "but how can we do that?"

"I don't see a problem," he answered. "We'll just take the radios."

So to a celebration dinner we went. The host seated us at a quiet little table for two. He lit the candle and wished us an enjoyable evening. Before getting completely settled, my husband reached into his pocket and pulled out the radio.

"Now," he said, carefully laying the walkie-talkie radio on the table, "we can eat together and not have to worry about all the others. They can reach us if we are needed!"

Our waiter approached and asked if we were ready to order. Eyeing the radio, he asked, "Is everything all right?"

"Oh, sure," my husband said. "This is our anniversary. We couldn't come out to dinner unless we brought all 132 of our *children* with us!"

 Aren't we glad we don't have 132 children to keep up with all the time? However, you are such a good father, I am sure you could handle it well!

LOVE NOTE HINT: If you have children, leave a note pointing out a time when you saw your spouse doing some exceptionally good parenting and the feelings you had as an observer. If you don't have children, remind your spouse of a time when he interacted with a niece, nephew, or child in the neighborhood, and tell him what a neat memory that is for you.

RECORDING MEMORIES

"Have you packed everything, Sweetheart?"

"I think so. I have our bathing suits, our pj's, some shorts, a sweater in case it is cool . . . ."

"I'm sure you got the normal stuff, but did you get our notebook and enough pens and paper? This has been a really busy year."

A notebook, paper, and pens on your anniversary trip?

Meg and Jonathan have been married for nine years, and every year they take a trip to celebrate their anniversary. From the beginning of their marriage, they have saved a few hours during each trip to reminisce and record their marriage and family highlights for that year. Some years, the exercise took no more than a couple of hours; other years, it required most of the day. Even so, *every* year they have been glad they took the time to do it. Throughout the years, they have been able to reread their entries and realize how God has had His hand on their family.

For instance, June 23, 2003, reads:

What a year! We had no idea this would be the year of so many blessings!

First was John's promotion to CEO of the company. He was surprised to be considered for that position so soon. We had been trusting God that when the time was right He would make that happen. Wow! A new schedule and so many new responsibilities.

Brian started first grade and Jake entered kindergarten. Everyone is doing great and learning so much every year.

Then, on May 14 our lives were changed in a big way when the twins were born. I couldn't even imagine keeping up with two more babies. But an even bigger surprise than their arrival was how much we are all enjoying these two precious little ones. Even though our schedule is busy, we love doing things together. The boys help me so much with Alice and Felicia. Already they recognize their voices and turn to look at them when they come into the room.

We feel like our family is complete and ask God each day to help us be the best parents we can possibly be. We are so thankful for this busy year. We trust Him with everything that happens in our lives. We are His.

LOVE NOTE HINT: Take time to talk or write about your year. How has God blessed you? Did you accomplish all your goals for your family? Talk about some ways you could make things even more meaningful for the next year.

Albert and Pat kept a family calendar on the refrigerator for years. It was large, and each day had plenty of room to write the things that were going on with their family and children. When extra space was available, Albert and Pat wrote notes to each other.

One Sunday's entry from Pat said, "I am so thankful God gave me a man who loves Him and is such a wonderful spiritual head for our family."

Albert wrote on a Saturday filled with soccer games, "I'm so thankful for you. I know you don't even like soccer, but you sit in the stands every weekend, cheering for our children. That is the sign of a wonderful mom."

Albert died several years ago, but Pat still has the calendars with 35 years worth of love notes—memories that are very precious to her. "I often get the calendars out and read them over again. Our grown children love to show them to their husbands and children. How thankful I am we took time to write calendar love notes to each other, on special days and every day."

No matter what day it is, you are special to me.

LOVE NOTE HINT: *Purchase a calendar with large empty blocks. Write down something nice your spouse did for you. It may be a very simple act of service or a way he provided a break when noticing how tired you were. Do this for a year, and give it to him as your anniversary card. This special memento will show how much you appreciate your mate every day of the year.*

GREAT GETAWAYS

Anniversaries are a great time to escape your normal routine. This year, plan a surprise getaway. Pick a destination and book the best room you can afford. Choose a destination you both will enjoy. Don't worry about "lots of things to do." This getaway is for you to have time together. After your husband leaves for work, pack a bag for the two of you. If possible, arrange with his boss for you to pick him up a little early from work. If not, be waiting with suitcases by the back door. If you want it to be a total surprise, don't tell him the destination. Either you drive or you be the navigator and give him only one instruction at a time. If possible, arrange to have a welcome surprise in the room for him: a small gift, flowers, his favorite snacks. This will be an anniversary he will never forget.

One year Christi and Lee couldn't get away because her mother was having major surgery the day before their anniversary.

"We were actually not able to celebrate until months later," Christi says. "But Lee made plans for a trip to a wonderful hotel to be taken on the date of my choice. He downloaded the logo for the hotel and made a gift certificate. It really looked professional."

Even though Christi and Lee did not get to celebrate their July anniversary until November, it was a trip well worth the wait.

When a couple cannot possibly get away on their anniversary, the day can still be remembered in a special way.

FAVORITE THINGS

Carmen is not a big lover of chocolate. She prefers sour candy. Her favorite is a candy called Sour Patch Kids, and her husband, Gary, just *had* to know it. During their five years of dating prior to marriage, Carmen told Gary about her preference many times.

On Carmen and Gary's first wedding anniversary, she was perplexed to receive from Gary a giant box inscribed Godiva Chocolatier. How could he forget that she really didn't care for chocolate? Carmen was really disappointed. She was glad Gary had not forgotten their anniversary, and the box was really beautiful . . . but she was still disappointed at the thought of Gary giving her *chocolate* for their anniversary.

Pulling the ribbon from the exquisite box, Carmen tried to figure out what to say that wouldn't crush him or be a total lie. She was really not excited about Gary's apparent choice of anniversary gifts.

Imagine Carmen's delight when she opened the lid, pulled back the paper covering, and found the box filled with Sour Patch Kids. Her husband had bought the chocolates, eaten them all (what a love note), bought her preferred candy in bulk, and pretended he was giving her a big box of chocolate. He probably gained five pounds in the process.

LOVE NOTE HINT: *Sometimes the gifts that aren't what they appear to be are the best surprises of all.*

PROGRESSIVE CELEBRATIONS

On Kelly and Trip's eighth anniversary, Kelly came home to an empty house. Her husband, Trip, would be home later. When she came in the back door, she found a single rose with a card on the kitchen table. "I love you for being such a wonderful cook," the card read.

Kelly put her stuff on the counter and continued toward the family room. There she saw another single rose with a card: "Thank you for being the financial mind of our family."

She took her son into his room to hang up his coat, and another rose with a message was spotted: "I love you for being such a wonderful mother to our son."

Everywhere in the house Kelly went, she saw more roses with love notes: "Thank you for being my best friend." "I love you for being such a beautiful woman." "Thank you for being so kind and thoughtful to others."

Finally, she found rose number eight on her bed. "Thank you most of all for being you. I love you," the card said.

You are a beautiful rose in my life's garden.

Thirty days before their thirtieth anniversary, Virginia received a card from Cecil that said, "We've had thirty wonderful years together. For the next thirty days, you will receive a gift from me."

For thirty days, Virginia received a gift each day. Some of them were Christmas ornaments to add to her Precious Moments collection; some were flowers or other items chosen especially for Virginia. On the thirtieth day, their anniversary, Virginia received thirty red roses. Her anniversary celebration that year was memorable and very special.

The local florist was so impressed that he began to spread the word, and others began to copy Cecil's idea for a special celebration. His love notes were not only a precious message to his wife, but also an inspiration to others.

LOVE NOTE HINT: When you choose to give several gifts spread out over a certain time period, the daily gifts don't have to be large. My mother always taught me it's the thought that counts. Multiple tokens of affection, even if individually small, will be welcome and memorable.

FAVORITE ANNIVERSARY GIFT

I have to tell you about one of my favorite anniversary gifts. My husband is the mover in the family. If I decided to rearrange the furniture, I would wait for my husband to come home to move heavy things around.

One year on our anniversary, he came in with a very large gift wrapped in about three large garbage bags. I couldn't imagine what he had for me. When I opened it, I was both surprised and delighted to find my own personal hand truck. Was it a frilly gift? No, not at all. Was it useful? Absolutely. In the many years since I received it, that hand truck has traveled with me many places, helped me move furniture, and, on occasion, helped move children into college and out again. It is probably the most practical gift I have ever received.

My husband remembers very well his favorite anniversary gift. He had just begun to hunt when a new hunting and game preserve opened in our area. I visited the preserve and looked at all their hunting packages. For our anniversary, I gave John a hunting package for three. He was able to take two friends and spend the day hunting. Because he was new to the sport, he learned a lot from the hunting club guides that day. That knowledge benefits him every year as he goes back out in the field.

MORE ANNIVERSARY IDEAS

♥ For an inexpensive but meaningful anniversary gift, make your husband a coloring book. Yes, you read it right, a coloring book! Look back through the pictures of places you have been together. Trace a landmark related to each place, using only the most important outlines. Draw one landmark per page. If necessary, enlarge the picture on a copier. If you have a comment that would add sentimentality, put that in large bold print. If you are skilled with a digital camera and the computer, you can use those tools to help you create a more professional-looking book.

The first coloring book I ever made was done by hand using a light bulb under the paper to help with tracing and a copy machine at work to enlarge the amateur images.

If you have children, you may want to make extra copies. They might like to color along, and it will be easier and more enjoyable if they have their own book.

♥ Make a card or purchase one with lots of space to write. Do a search at the library or on the Internet to find the words for *I love you* in as many other languages as possible. Confess your love to your spouse in as many different languages as space allows. For example:

Et tu amo	Portuguese
Nakupenda	Swahili
Te Amo	Spanish
Wo ie ni	Chinese
Je t'aime	French
Ti Amo	Italian

For a variation on this idea, write your spouse a love letter and have someone translate it into another language. With the letter, provide a small dictionary for that language, and let him translate the letter back to English.

♥ If you find you have to be out of town on your special day, arrange for love notes to be delivered to your spouse throughout the day. These surprises can come in the form of phone calls, letters (be sure to mail them in time to arrive on the correct day), flowers, gifts, or even unexpected visits from friends.

Birthdays

MAKE A SCRAPBOOK

Scrapbooking is in; it is a wonderful way to document those special times or events in our lives. Scrapbooking, however, is not a new hobby. In my attic, I have my mother's scrapbooks. From the time she met my dad throughout their time together, she saved everything. She kept even the paper from the straw he drank from, napkins he used to wipe his mouth, a string he used to tie a package. Of course, she also saved some of the normal fare, such as pictures, movie stubs, and dead flowers, which are now more than half a century old.

When my sister and I cleaned out Mom's house, we didn't know what to do with those scrapbooks. They were much too precious to discard. Sister and I sat and looked through each page that had lovingly been designed. Everything that was pasted on the pages was a testimony of my mother's love for my father. I am sure he was amazed the first time she showed him the scrapbooks at how many things she kept just because he had touched them!

Dena also likes to preserve her family memories in a scrapbook. "I love to scrapbook," says Dena, "and sometimes I will make a mini-scrapbook of pictures and memories from one event, like an anniversary or a trip. It's a thoughtful, fun, inexpensive, handmade gift . . . one that is always treasured.

"When our children were old enough, I involved them in scrapbook making for their father. Last year for my hubby's birthday, my son, Jordan, made a construction paper booklet of drawings and simple sentences about "Why I love my Dad," and we used yarn to tie it all together. It was his dad's favorite gift."

LOVE NOTE HINT: *Make a small scrapbook of things you really enjoy doing together. If you like to dine out or order take-out meals, make a scrapbook of menus from all the places you like to eat. If movies are what you enjoy together, clip ads for the movies you see and put them in a scrapbook along with the ticket stubs. For an outdoors couple, saving leaves or flowers from hikes or camping trips could make for pleasant reminiscing.*

RESEARCH THE DAY

Several days or weeks before your mate's birthday, spend a few hours in the library. Search for the headlines from the day he was born. Use the Internet to find other persons who share his birthday. Find special events that took place on his birthday. Was that the day popcorn was first popped? If so, celebrate with a big bag of popcorn. Some stores even sell booklets with all the information you would need to create a memorable and nostalgic birthday.

A lot of special things may have happened on this day, but the best one of all was your birth!

Tony Dale is an author, songwriter, and poet. For his wife's birthday, he usually buys a gift. However, of all the gifts he gives her, the most special are the ones he *writes* for her. Here is one birthday poem he wrote for her:

> No man has ever been more blessed,
> Paired as I with such a mate,
> Truly meant to fit with me
> From the moment you drew breath.
>
> I thank the Lord that you were born
> Upon this day so far away,
> That through His wisdom He would place
> You, my love, with me this day.
> —Tony Dale, 05/20/05

CELEBRATE SOMEONE ELSE'S SPECIAL OCCASION
Someone else's birthday can be an occasion for celebration as well.

Cecil and Virginia wanted to get a very special gift for their daughter to celebrate her twenty-first birthday. They visited several jewelry stores and looked for that one-of-a-kind item that would make the day special. While they were browsing through one of the jeweler's cases, Virginia found a bracelet she really liked. They talked about it a lot, but weren't quite sure they should get it for Celia, their daughter. They eventually ended up getting something else for the birthday gift.

Celia was in college in a different town, so they planned an overnight trip to visit her. On the morning of her birthday, they drove the hour and a half to spend the day with her. They had a wonderful day and enjoyed being with their only daughter.

When they went to the car the next day to head back home, Virginia saw a small gift in her seat. It was the bracelet Virginia had so admired when shopping for Celia's gift. Cecil had purchased the bracelet as a present for Virginia in celebration of Celia's twenty-first birthday!

Virginia says of that bracelet, "That gift really touched me. I wear it proudly now as a token of his love and as a reminder of the day our *baby* turned 21."

LOVE NOTE HINT: *Turn someone else's special occasion into an opportunity to say "I love you" to your spouse. Just be sure not to take the focus off of the honoree of the day.*

SURPRISE ON THE JOB

Tina teaches school. Because her birthday happens during the school year, her husband, John, does not have much opportunity to take her out to lunch for her birthday. One year he decided to change that.

Before her class was scheduled to come into the cafeteria, John came to the school, went to the cafeteria, and set up Tina's class's table with tablecloth, candles, and balloons—the whole works. When Tina and her class walked in, they were really excited. They had never seen a table in the lunchroom look so beautiful. John's birthday love note to Tina was talked about for a long time by that third grade class!

Valentine's Day

HOW DO I LOVE THEE?

It's never financially easy when you are married and in college. That was just the case for Anne and her husband, John. It was Valentine's Day, and no money was available, even for a card.

Anne baked a few cookies with the ingredients she had on hand. Then she found a scrap of red poster board and cut it into a two-by-two-inch square. On the square, she drew a little Martian face caricature, as was popular in the 1960s.

While Anne was working on her valentine items, John initiated a plan of his own. He went to the library and collected love quotes from famous poets. After cutting some paper into ten squares of identical size, he wrote a quote along with a personal thought on each square.

For instance, if the quote was "How do I love thee? Let me count the ways," he made a numbered list of the things he loved about Anne. John then connected all the squares together, side by side, with packing tape, folded them into a stack so they looked like only one square, and wrapped his creation. John proudly presented this unique beautifully wrapped gift to Anne. When she unwrapped it and picked up the top square, the stack unfolded with John's elongated declaration of love for her. Needless to say, that card is Anne's most cherished Valentine's Day card.

WILD THING

Jim's most memorable valentine came in the form of a balloon bouquet.

His wife, Candy, sent the balloon bouquet to him at work. The shiny Mylar balloon in the middle said, "Wild Thing."

"At first I think it embarrassed him," said Candy, "but he got lots of comments from the guys. I think they were a little jealous!"

Jim must have really liked it, too. When Valentine's Day was over, he brought the Wild Thing balloon home and mounted it on the back of their bedroom door. Later he returned the thought when he presented Candy with a stuffed gorilla that played "Wild Thing."

MORE VALENTINE CARD IDEAS

♥ Make a giant card. Begin by folding a regular sized piece of poster paper in half. Find some old magazines, and cut out cartoons and advertisements that remind you of things your husband likes. Glue them on the front of the card as a collage of his special interests. Also find your name spelled out in print to mix into the collage. On the inside, write a special message and refer to some of the items on the front. My husband still has a similar card I made for him over three decades ago.

♥ Buy a composition book, a colorful binder, or a pretty notebook. Make an alphabet notebook, with one page for each letter in the alphabet. Write words for each letter that describe your mate. If you want to write more than a few words, begin a love letter with the letter on the page. You might even combine the two ideas. For example: A—Awesome; All my life I looked for a husband as wonderful as you.

Mother's Day

Bette and Kevin had been married a year and a half when he surprised her with a beautiful Mother's Day card. He put it under her pillow Mother's Day night. Bette wasn't expecting anything for Mother's Day, since they had no children yet. But when she was getting ready for bed Sunday night and fluffed her pillow, there it was.

Bette says, "It was the most beautiful gesture of love and excitement about our future family. He talked about my ability to be a good mother since I take care of him so well. That really meant a lot."

Will had watched Elizabeth silently endure many short, tepid showers on school mornings when she was the last to bathe. With all their children, hot water ran out quickly in the morning.

One Mother's Day, Will decided to do something about Elizabeth's hot water predicament. For her Mother's Day gift, he bought a new hot water heater and had it installed in their bathroom. Now she has all the hot water she needs no matter how many family members bathe before her.

"That was truly a love note to me," she says. "I don't have to worry about hot water any more!"

Thanksgiving

Many years when our children were small, we made a Thanksgiving tree for our den wall. I made a crude, but recognizable, tree trunk out of brown construction paper and taped it to the wall. Then we cut or tore leaves out of the fall-colored paper, wrote the names of family members for whom we were thankful, and taped them to the tree. Our tree brightened up an otherwise blank wall for a month and served as a reminder of our wonderful family every time we passed it.

Now that the children are older, the Thanksgiving tree has moved, and its leaves serve a new purpose—love noting to my husband. The trunk is taped to the mirror above my husband's sink. Each day I add a new leaf:

Day 1—I am thankful for you.

Day 2—I am thankful God brought us together.

Day 3—I am thankful you are my husband.

Day 4—I am thankful you are so thoughtful. Thank you for taking out the trash every week.

Day 5—I am thankful you like to watch movies
with me.

Day 6—I am thankful you love God.

Day 7—I am thankful . . .

*LOVE NOTE HINT: Prepare a Thanksgiving basket for your
mate, and put it at his place at the table or by his bathroom
sink. Pack it full of things that show him how much you appreciate him. Include a new book by his favorite author, a bottle
of massage oil if he enjoys an occasional massage, a small pack
of his favorite flavor or brand of coffee, coupons for dinner at
a restaurant he likes. He will feel special and appreciated when
he realizes how personalized each item in the basket is.*

C hristmas

"I LOVE YOU FOR THAT" BOOK

Caz wanted to have a very special Christmas present for
Leslie. Early in the year, he began writing a book that
would be her Christmas present. The book was entitled,
I Love You for That! On each of the 365 pages, he wrote
something that he loved about Leslie. Each entry ended
with "I Love You for That!"

The gift was a hit. Even though she was supposed to
make it last all year, Leslie read it in just a few months.
She enjoyed every comment and savored the memory
of the subject of each day. Now, on days when Caz is

out of town, Leslie can curl up in her favorite chair, reread a page of the book, and feel his presence right there with her.

LOVE NOTE HINT: Write a book for your love. Create one page for each day of the year. If you want to make it interactive, use a notebook large enough for your spouse to write back to you for the following year.

TWELVE DAYS OF LOVE NOTING

Will and Elizabeth have been married for over thirty years. For most of those years, they have tried to find creative ways to say "I love you" to each other.

One year Will had an interesting idea. Drawing inspiration from the "The Twelve Days of Christmas" song, he decided to do something special for Elizabeth each of the 12 days *before* Christmas. Sometimes it was just a silly little gift, sometimes it was a lasting token of love, sometimes it was a note that conveyed the message of the day, but always it carried the message "You are special. I love you at Christmas and all year long." This idea was carried out many years. Looking at Will's gifting for one of those years gives a good picture of his creativity.

On the first day of Christmas: Elizabeth's favorite place to vacation was the beach. When she opened the door to the bathroom on the morning of the first day of Christmas, she was greeted by a bathroom transformed into a beach! Will had sneaked into their oversized bathroom after Elizabeth had gone to bed and set up the beach umbrella and beach chairs, spread out the beach towels, strategically placed a few beach balls, and even provided a little sand. (Will went all out with this one.) Her chair contained a new book to read and her drink holder held her favorite beverage.

Love Note: Life with you is like a day at the beach—wonderful in every way. Merry First Day of Christmas.

On the second day of Christmas: A pair of earrings was the gift of the day; it was a gold pair Elizabeth had admired in the store.

Love Note: Our love is more precious than gold.

On the third day of Christmas: The third morning, Elizabeth found three magazines tied with a bow at her place at the table.

Love Note: Take a moment to relax today and enjoy these.

On the fourth day of Christmas: In "The Twelve Days of Christmas" song, the gift for the fourth day is four calling birds. For this fourth day of Christmas, Elizabeth received four unusual telephone calls to wish her a happy day: one from Robin, one from Wren, one from Mrs. Parrott, and one from Miss Crow. She had her own personal *calling birds*!

Love Note: I am so thankful to be able to call you my wife. I am blessed.

On the fifth day of Christmas: The five golden rings, as called for in the song, were replaced by five Butterfinger bars, Elizabeth's favorite candy.

Love Note: Five Butterfingers, one for each day, each with a message, I love you today!

On the sixth day of Christmas: Will and Elizabeth have six children; so for the sixth day of Christmas, Elizabeth received a new individual picture of each child to display on their family wall.

Love Note: Each one of these pictures represents a very special gift from God. I love each of them very much, and I love their mother.

On the seventh day of Christmas: When Elizabeth wants to sit by the fire and read a book, she loves to have a cup of tea. In celebration of the seventh day, she received a pretty new mug with seven tea bags.

Love Note: Enjoy a cup of tea. If you could read the tea leaves, they would say, "I love you!"

On the eighth day of Christmas: Eight tickets for a special Christmas program provided a special night out for Elizabeth and her entire family.

Love Note: I am so proud when I go out in public with you and our precious family.

On the ninth day of Christmas: Will hid nine small presents for Elizabeth all over the house. The first one was revealed at nine o'clock in the morning. The phone rang; it was a friend. "Will said for you to go look in the cookie jar on the kitchen cabinet," she said.

When Elizabeth got to the cookie jar, she found a Christmas pad of paper and a note. "A song is not a song until you sing it, a pad is of no use unless you have something to write with! Go look in the top secretary drawer in the living room."

Elizabeth, following the instructions, found a pen that matched her new notepad. The accompanying note said, "At the next strike of the grandfather clock, watch it chime as you listen." At the top of the next hour, Elizabeth went to the grandfather clock and there, tied to the top, was a small box. When she opened it, she found a pretty pin to wear.

This gifting adventure continued until nine o'clock that night. The note discovered last had said, "At the chiming of the hour, look for your personal Santa. He'll be dressed in red and ready to give you a back rub." At that time, Will, dressed in his red pajamas, lit candles, put on soft music, and gave Elizabeth a wonderful back rub. The ninth day of Christmas was very special.

On the tenth day of Christmas: Elizabeth loves fountain sodas from a particular restaurant. Almost every morning after she takes the children to school, she drives through that restaurant's take-out window and orders one soda. For the tenth day of Christmas, Will went to the restaurant and paid for ten fountain drinks. For the next ten days, all Elizabeth had to do was pull up to the window and collect her treat!

Love Note: I will be thinking of you as you start your day!

On the eleventh day of Christmas: Eleven peppermints of her favorite kind were given to her in a festive bag.

Love Note: Peppermints enough to share, peppermints to show I care, peppermints for you to eat, peppermints for you, my sweet!

On the twelfth day of Christmas: Twelve chocolate KISSES wrapped in Christmas colors were the gift of the day.

Love Note: Available any season, twelve real kisses just for you.

Some years, Elizabeth turned the tables and treated Will to a celebration of the twelve days leading up to Christmas. The following is an example of her gifting one such year.

On the first day of Christmas: Elizabeth bought Will a new pine bench for their garden. On the back of the bench sat an artificial partridge.

Love Note: I'd sit by the partridge on a pine tree with you any day.

On the second day of Christmas: Will's favorite dessert is chocolate; so for this second day of Christmas, Elizabeth baked a *double* chocolate cake. This treat actually lasted several days.

Love Note: Twice as much chocolate is always better. You are twice as much fun to be with as anyone else I know!

―――――――――――――

On the third day of Christmas: Will often plays Santa during the holidays, and he gardens in the summer. On this third day, Elizabeth presented him with (1) a hoe, (2) a trowel, and (3) a spade, as well as a note to playfully make connection between the tools and his Santa activities.

Love Note: Hoe, hoe, hoe!

―――――――――――――

On the fourth day of Christmas: Elizabeth gave Will four of his favorite candy bars for this day.

Love Note: If it wasn't 4 you, life would be boring! I thank God every day 4 creating us 4 each other.

―――――――――――――

On the fifth day of Christmas: Not to be outdone by Will's four calling birds (mentioned earlier), Elizabeth arranged for Will to receive five telephone calls (*rings*) on this fifth day. Each of the calls was from a couple who had been married at least 50 years. Each shared with Will best wishes for the holidays and a tidbit about their own Christmas tradition.

Love Note: I love the Christmas traditions we have established in our family, especially _____ _____ (You could insert your favorite tradition here). I hope we can continue it for many years to come.

On the sixth day of Christmas: Will also likes to collect coins. Several nights a week he cleans out his pockets and puts his newly found treasures in his coin books. Elizabeth gave him six coins on the sixth day and hoped they were ones he didn't already have.

Love Note: You are worth more than gold or silver to me.

On the seventh day of Christmas: Elizabeth decided to branch out on the seventh day. While Will was at lunch she went by his office and left seven chocolate KISSES and seven chocolate HUGS.

Love Note: Seven is the perfect number, and I think you are just perfect for me! (You may collect seven real hugs and kisses when you get home!)

On the eighth day of Christmas: Elizabeth gave Will a copy of part of the Christmas story, Luke 2 beginning with verse 8 (of course) and continuing through verse 20 (the shepherds' experience).

Love Note: I am so thankful that you are the spiritual leader of our home and teach our children about the real meaning of Christmas.

On the ninth day of Christmas: The "nine ladies dancing" need music to dance to, so Elizabeth found nine of Will's favorite songs and put them on a CD for him.

Love Note: I know on the ninth day the gift should be nine ladies dancing, but I don't want anyone dancing with you except me! How 'bout a dancing date?

On the tenth day of Christmas: Will enjoys going to the movies, so Elizabeth gave him ten movie passes. She was in hopes that he would ask her to accompany him to see some of the movies.

Love Note: You are the star of all the movies of my dreams!

On the eleventh day of Christmas: Will loves tools, so to highlight the eleventh day of Christmas, Elizabeth gave him a new drill with ten drill bits. He was thrilled and couldn't wait for Elizabeth to give him a new project. Elizabeth was hoping he would say that.

Love Note: Here's a drill. I love you to bits!

On the twelfth day of Christmas: Christmas Eve is always special at Elizabeth and Will's house. For years, they have found themselves staying up late to fill stockings and put toys together. Even when their children got older, it seemed like so much still needed to be done at the last minute before the Christmas Day festivities. Elizabeth's twelfth day gift for Will was her own version of Christmas peace.

Love Note: At the stroke of midnight, you have my undivided attention, even if all the stockings aren't ready yet!

A CHRISTMAS CATALOG

Christi is a stay-at-home mom to two-year-old Morgan. Her husband, Lee, knows that Christi would much rather spend money on Morgan than on herself. Whenever Christi goes shopping for Morgan, Lee always tells her to be sure to get something for herself. Christi rarely does that because she tries very hard to spend their money only on true *needs* and save as much as possible. Christi clips coupons and loves bargain shopping.

One Christmas, Lee's gift was particularly heart-warming. The card on this particular package said, "For Mommy, Love, Morgan." Lee saved it as the last gift to be opened at the family Christmas. As Morgan helped open the gift, Christi saw the front cover of a booklet entitled, "Christi's Shopping Catalog." Lee had down-loaded images of a popular clothing line and created Christi's own personal catalog. In the back of this catalog were three gift certificates: One entitled Christi to lunch, dinner, and a shopping spree on a particular date. Another was for the usual babysitter to provide childcare from 9:00 A.M. until 2:00 P.M. (Lee had pre-arranged the date with the babysitter!). The third gift certificate was signed by Christi's mother; it was for babysitting from 2:00 until they returned that evening.

It was obvious Lee had spent many hours working on creating the beautiful color catalog. However, as impressed as Christi was with his creativity and computer graphic skills, she was overwhelmed with love and thank-fulness for the man who took such pleasure in trying to make her happy. His enclosed note said he wanted to give her something to thank her for being his loving wife and a devoted mother to their daughter.

No coat, purse, or pair of shoes could come close in comparison to the priceless gift of that *love note* in the form of a computer-generated catalog with gift certificates. That love note celebrated the love, respect, and admiration Christi and Lee share for one another; that was the greatest gift Lee could have given Christi.

STOCKINGS FROM SANTA

Before John and I had children, we filled Christmas stockings for each other. We shopped all year for bargains to fill the stockings. When the children came along, we continued our tradition. After the children were in bed, we fixed our stockings for each other, enjoyed opening them, and then repositioned them in the playroom with all the other gifts Santa had brought. For many years, our children thought Santa came to see Mom and Dad, too.

This tradition actually began in my family when I was a little girl. When I was a preteen, I talked to my brother and sister and convinced them that if we tried very hard, we could fix stockings for our parents, and they would think Santa had decided to include them, too.

For years we sneaked around, wanting to make sure we weren't caught. Our parents always played along. When we first started to do this, my brother was only about four years old. He took tremendous delight in thinking we had fooled our parents. We all enjoyed watching him and shared his excitement as he watched our parents discover what was in their stockings.

Now that we are the parents, we still play the game and our older children always want to see what Santa brought us!

LOVE NOTE HINT: Even if you don't fix stockings for each other, take time to include a few special surprises for each other during this special season.

A CHRISTMAS RING

Some Christmas love notes are lasting: not only precious gifts for the moment, but also treasures for years to come.

Edna was experiencing the first Christmas season since her husband's death, and it had thus far been very difficult despite her desire to focus on the real meaning of the season.

On Christmas Day, Edna heard a knock at her door. There stood a man she recognized, a local jeweler, bundled up in his winter coat. In his hand was a beautifully wrapped package. It was a gift for Edna. She couldn't imagine who had sent her the gift, but she thanked the man and took the box.

Going inside, she sat down on the sofa to open it.

Her daughter came into the room and asked, "What's that, Mom?"

"I don't know," Edna said. "Mr. Jackson from the jewelry store just delivered it."

"Well, open it," her daughter said. "Let's see who sent you a present . . . from the jewelry store at that!"

Edna carefully opened the box, and a card slipped out. Taking it out of the little envelope, Edna read, "Wish I could be with you. I am there in spirit, and I will always love you." It was from her husband.

Edna's husband had died several months earlier. He had known for a long time that his condition was terminal. Even as he prepared himself to go to heaven to be with Jesus, he was thinking of his wife whom he loved dearly. At some point before he died, he had gone by the jewelry store and picked out a special gift to be delivered at Christmas after his death.

In the box was a beautiful gold ring, a simple style that Edna's husband knew she would like. It was engraved with the words "Love you forever."

LOVE NOTE HINT: Plan ahead. You don't have to wait until you are gone to surprise your spouse with a lovely reminder of your commitment. Sit down today and write a long love letter— the kind you used to write when you were engaged.

Chapter Four

Love Notes for Other Special Days

Before You Are Married

I am prone to lose things. Recently, I had to locate a very important paper. Finding it required that I clean out some places that I rarely visit—among them, the drawer in the nightstand by my bed.

As I sifted through more than forty years of memories, I came across several notes I had placed in the drawer before I had a special spot reserved for my love notes. These pieces of paper were yellow and dog-eared.

One note brought back very special memories. I had just met my husband-to-be, John, although at that time, I didn't know that was the case. My family and I had gone out of town during my spring break from college. John drove all the way to my hometown to surprise me with a visit, but he was the one surprised when I was not home.

Our family returned home on Saturday, so we could be in church on Easter Sunday. There on the back porch sat a giant Easter basket. The attached note read, "Happy Easter! May your day be bright and sunny and all your eggs be found. See you back at school on Tuesday." It was signed, Easter Bunny.

News spread quickly about my surprise visit from the Easter Bunny, and for several years, people in my hometown asked me if I was still dating the Easter Bunny.

LOVE NOTE HINT: *Any day can be a special occasion. Recognize the holidays, but if you need an excuse to celebrate, create your own or look at the calendar. There is a day for almost everything now: National Peanut Butter Lovers Day (March 1), National Popcorn Month (October), Get a New Toothbrush Day (February 13), and the list goes on.*

"I am a long-time journaler," says Dena. "I think I was 11 when I began writing in my little wire-bound notebooks. As I got older, I realized the importance of praying for my future husband, whoever and wherever he was. When my hubby-to-be and I got engaged, I gave him a collection of all the prayers I had prayed for him, gleaned from the many journals I had kept since I was 11. He loved it! It made him realize how much I had anticipated our life together, even when I didn't know his name."

Pillow Talk:

Think back to before you were married. What were the things that attracted you to your mate? Pick one and applaud it in a note on his pillow.

The Day You Met

Reserve the anniversary of the day you first met to take a walk down memory lane. Go out to dinner and reminisce about that first time together. What did you think of each other? What did you talk about? If you still live in that town, visit the place you went on that first date. If you are not in the same town, plan a trip there in the future.

Milestone event anniversaries are not always easy for husbands to remember. Usually they have little trouble with wedding anniversaries, but do not normally take note of every little milestone in a relationship.

My husband and I met on March 30. I doubt he could tell you what date we met, even after many reminders that March 30 is a special day. Our first date was a blind date, though prior to that date I had actually declared that I was not going to go on any more blind dates.

However, my friend, who lived across the hall from me in the dorm, came to my room. Her older sister had three friends who had just decided they might like to go out on Saturday night and wanted her to "fix them up." This phone call came to my friend at 3:30 on Saturday afternoon (yes, the same Saturday afternoon we were to go out). My friend really wanted me to accept a blind date with this friend of her sister.

I immediately said no! I had tried the blind date thing before, and it hadn't been much fun. I was perfectly happy entertaining myself on Saturday night. But my friend told me that this was no ordinary blind date; this guy was really nice, something *extremely* special. I guess these days she would have said, "He's really hot!"

She convinced me to go, and later, I agreed with her. This guy was something special. I enjoyed his company and our conversation. After dinner, we went to the apartment of a friend and watched a black-and-white movie about pollution. (I know, that doesn't sound very romantic. And yes, we did have color television back then!) I didn't like to watch movies, but I pretended to be very interested. After all, he seemed to be enjoying it. Over the years, that pollution movie has probably been one of the most talked about movies in history; however, neither one of us can remember the name. I can describe scenes in the movie to this day and remember how hard it was to seem interested.

We didn't date steadily until more than a year later; still each March 30, we talk about that *first* date. That day is not only remembered as the day we met, but also as "pollution movie day!" I hope someday to be able to find that movie to commemorate our first date.

Pillow Talk

I'm glad I took a chance on one more blind date!

First Days

Sometimes it is more fun to create your own special days—days that have meaning just within your family. Some of these might include celebrating the anniversary of the day you met, your first date, and day of your engagement. You could celebrate your first day in your new house, at a new job, or driving a new car.

Polly and Mark celebrate the first day of every month as a special occasion.

"We each try to be the first one to wish the other 'Happy June' or 'Happy November' when the first day of the month comes around," Polly says.

Polly and Mark have gotten quite creative with their first-of-the-month ideas. Some months, one of them sets his or her alarm for 12:01 A.M. in order to be the first one to deliver wishes. Sometimes a note is written on the mirror, so it will be seen immediately upon arising. Messages on cell phones have also been another of their favorite ways to wish each other a happy first-of-the-month day.

"We love to celebrate the arrival of another month and thank God for His continued care over us and our family," says Polly. "It reminds us that every day is a gift from God and one to be cherished. We always end with the words, "I love you," as we enter a new month together."

A very simple thing to do? Yes. And a lot of fun. They have built a special tradition for their family that is sure to continue. Now that they have children, the children often get in the game! They send reminders to their parents to be sure they don't forget to wish each other a happy month.

LOVE NOTE HINT: Have a standing date the first day of every week. Reserve Sunday nights to be together. After church, make a special Sunday night dinner, complete with candles, soft music, and linen napkins. Take time to connect before entering another hectic week.

Tuesday Gifts

I have heard of a wonderful English tradition called the Tuesday gift. A Tuesday gift is a little gift given for no reason. The gift doesn't have to be big to be meaningful. Sometimes you could be like the Brits and get your man a Tuesday gift. Leave it on the seat of his car or drop it on his desk while he is out to lunch.

Your Tuesday gift could be a gift of time. When you know he is going to have the afternoon off, arrange to be at home yourself. Spend some quality time together before school is out. Make a dream list of things you want to do together. Post your number one dream on the dresser mirror to remind you often of something you really want to do together some day.

In Sickness

Sharon's husband put love notes on her pillow every day for nine years.

Before the love noting started, when Sharon was 26 years old, she was struck with a debilitating case of major clinical depression. After five years of marriage, she was reduced from being an active wife, mother of two little girls, and volunteer worker to being a woman whose greatest accomplishments became getting showered and dressed in the morning. During the next nine years, Sharon spent eighty weeks as a patient in hospital psychiatric wards. When she was at home, she sometimes slept 18 hours a day as a result of fatigue from the antidepressant medications combined with a desire to escape life.

Tim stuck with Sharon through all that. When Sharon didn't think she could go on, he told her, "You will get better." He also promised, "I will always love you; I will never leave you." Her husband became "God with skin on" to her, a human demonstration of His love, throughout those difficult years.

Tim took their daughters to church each Sunday, even when Sharon was too ill to leave the house. As the girls, attired in dresses their daddy picked out for them, their hair braided by his hands, left with him to go to church, a note could be found on Sharon's pillow, saying something in the nature of "I love you enough to see that our daughters are raised to know their heavenly Father."

Christmases were particularly stressful during Sharon's depression. Tim and Sharon usually hosted a big family dinner in their home, but Sharon often became overwhelmed with plans, preparations, and people. Tim knew this. One year he offered to do everything. He made the entire Christmas dinner with all the family's favorite dishes; he set the table, served the meal, and attended to the guests.

When Sharon asked if she could help, Tim said, "No, you go rest. I'll take care of everything." His love note that night read, "Because I love you, I will serve you and those you love."

Tim's *action* love notes, such as making Christmas dinner and now a wonderful meal each Mother's Day, have become traditions.

How does a marriage survive when one of the partners has to do all the giving, receiving little in return? Sharon answers that question in her story, "A Mission of Love," published in *God Answers Prayers* (Harvest House, 2005): "Recently, I asked my husband what made him remain faithful to me during those dark years. His reply was very honest: 'While you were sick, it didn't really seem like we had a marriage relationship, so I just kept telling myself that you were my mission field, my ministry opportunity.'"

Sharon says that every morning when she awoke and her husband was still there, it was as though he had placed a love note on her pillow, saying, "Because you are so precious to me, I will sacrifice my own dreams, even my life, to take care of you."

Sharon has been free from depression for six years now. She says she will try to fill the rest of his life with love notes to him as beautiful as those he wrote and performed for her during those difficult years.

LOVE NOTE HINT: Sometimes it seems like a relationship is very one-sided. During those times when it seems that one person has to give more than the other, be sure to pray with and for each other. Cling to God as you cling to each other, and trust His faithfulness to bring you through the difficult times.

Because of a serious illness Miriam experienced when she was in her twenties, doctors told her that she would never be able to have or care for children. In spite of that dire prediction, Larrion and Miriam married and had four children together. In order to preserve his wife's health and give her a break from constant child care and chauffeuring, Larrion saved Friday nights to take his children roller-skating and Sunday afternoons to take them horseback riding, bicycling, or swimming. Sometimes he would even take all four kids to the beach for a weekend and leave Miriam to rest. These special times were love notes to his wife and created wonderful memories for their children.

Miriam says, "I would have never made it without him to relieve me and give me some peace and quiet!"

LOVE NOTE HINT: *If you and your spouse are in the midst of the child-raising years, look for ways you can relieve one another when a break is needed.*

Ray loved lobster. When he had an extended stay in the hospital, Esther realized that he must miss eating this delicacy. She also knew that lobster was not on the hospital's menu, so one afternoon she stopped by a seafood place and picked up an order of freshly steamed lobster. The look on his face when she walked in with this special treat made the extra trouble worthwhile. That lobster tail definitely said, "I love you."

Chapter Five

Paperless Love Notes

Love notes don't always have to be written on paper. Often the sweetest note comes in the form of an act of service, an unexpected gift, or a simple touch. Sometimes we don't even think of them as love notes.

Constantly make mental notes of the things your spouse does for you that mean a lot to you. Verbally thank him or her on the spot. It doesn't have to be something big. Even the most mundane tasks performed regularly and without prompting mean a lot. Reward your spouse with a word of encouragement the next time you notice one of those seemingly insignificant tasks being done.

Do you have a favorite tree out in the yard? After dinner one night, take a walk around your yard, and carve your initials in the trunk of a tree like they used to do. Carve a heart around them. As the tree grows, you will have a constant reminder of your love and your commitment to each other. Every time one of you cuts the grass, you will see the public declaration of your commitment to each other.

*M*irror Notes

Scott goes to work very early. He and his wife, Deb, don't usually see each other in the morning, so Deb likes to surprise Scott by leaving notes and small gifts in his truck.

One morning after Scott got in the truck, cranked it up, fastened his seat belt, and put it in gear, he looked in the rearview mirror and began to smile. There on the mirror in bright red lipstick were the words *I love you*. He knew that Deb had slipped outside after he had gone to bed and left him a special message for the morning. (*Hint: Lipstick can be easily removed with glass cleaner.*)

Lipstick also works well on the bathroom mirror. However, at our house, we learned the hard way to make sure it was totally removed.

Even though we have plenty of bathrooms, our children preferred using ours when they were growing up. I'm not quite sure whether it made them feel more a part of the family group or they just liked our bathroom better.

One day when one of our children took a shower in our bathroom, I heard a loud "Mom, come here! Mom!"

I couldn't imagine what was wrong. There stood our eight-year-old daughter wrapped in a towel, pointing at the mirror. The more steam that filled the room, the clearer my former message appeared. Apparently I had not used enough glass cleaner!

Fortunately, that message was not an X-rated one, but the next time I wrote on the mirror with lipstick, I made sure to clean and reclean that spot!

LOVE NOTE HINT: *Dry erase markers work well on mirrors and glass and are much easier to clean off!*

Cheryl and Clint live in a small house with only one bathroom. When they have somewhere to go at night, they often have to get ready at the same time.

Once Cheryl puts on the final touches, she usually stands in front of the full-length mirror and turns around once or twice.

Clint always makes the same comment, "Honey, you look really good."

Her reply is always the same as well. "I always want to look good for my man!"

Their little ritual during preparation for their evening sets the tone for a positive selfless date!

LOVE NOTE HINT: *When you are getting ready to go out and you and your spouse are in the bathroom primping, write him a message on the steamed up mirror or shower door.*

Simple Touches and Special Codes

For a number of years, Glenn was an anchorman on the television evening news. At the end of each broadcast, he touched the knot on his tie. What did that mean?

Touching the knot on his tie was a prearranged signal between Glenn and his wife, Rhonda, that meant, "I love you."

Did the viewers know this exchange went on at the end of every broadcast? Probably not. Did his wife get the message? Absolutely.

Carol Burnett also used a signal at the end of each of her television shows. Her fans will remember that after singing her closing theme song, she said good night to the audience and then pulled on her left earlobe. This tugging gesture was for her grandmother, Nanny, to let her know that everything was all right.

I have heard, too, that years ago, John Daly, moderator of the game show *What's My Line?* tugged on his ear when the panelist's conversation was getting a bit too risqué. That was the signal to change the subject.

One older couple at church can often be seen exchanging private messages in the form of squeezing each other's hand. Three squeezes represent the words *I love you*. Four squeezes mean *I love you, too*.

When the wife had to have heart surgery, she could not verbally communicate with her husband, so their wordless messaging was a comfort to them both. When the husband sat at her bedside and held her hand, she squeezed three times, and, of course, he always squeezed back.

LOVE NOTE HINT: *What kind of special signals do you send to your husband or wife? If you have not established any yet, initiate one and use it often.*

Early in their marriage, Maria began signing, "I love you," to Jack. If they were in public, she held it down by her side or on top of her pocket book.

Jack's return sign was simply two fingers held up, meaning, "I love you, too." When they were at home, it became a game, with Maria returning two fingers on one hand and one on the other. Then Jack held up two and two and so on.

For Jack, however, the number *two* became the secret sign of his love for Maria, and Maria often found it around the house and in her car. She knew when she saw the number two, it meant, "I love you, too."

Maria was away one weekend, and Jack decided to make her homecoming really special. He spent the afternoon decorating the house with welcome home signs and number twos. He even went so far as to decorate the yard and the cul-de-sac where they lived with twos.

As a final touch, Jack went out to the stop sign on the corner and affixed his last *two*. He carefully taped the number to the sign.

As he stepped back to admire his handiwork, he heard a car turn in the street behind him. The car stopped, and he heard the door slam. Turning around, he was greeted by a city policeman.

"Morning, sir," the policeman said. "Is there a problem here?"

"Oh, no," Jack said. "I am just decorating a little. My wife has been gone all weekend, and I wanted to welcome her home in a special way. She'll know what all this means."

"Oh, really? Well, do you know what this means for you to put that number on the stop sign?" the officer asked.

"Same as all the other twos. It means 'I love my wife.' She'll get the message."

"Well, it also means I am going to give you a ticket for defacing public property."

"What?" Jack replied. "It's only going to be there for a couple of hours, and the sign is not going to be hurt at all."

"Sorry, fellow, but there is a city ordinance about affixing anything to street signs. I am going to have to give you a ticket."

"You are kidding, right?"

"Nope, serious as I can be. I believe you have said enough about it, too, or I could add another violation."

"Officer, couldn't you just give me a warning? I'll take the sign down right now," Jack said.

"Sorry, pal," he said. "Laws are laws."

Jack's creative welcome home cost him a little more than his time, but Maria's exclamation when they drove in the street made it all worthwhile.

LOVE NOTE HINT: Think of some sort of secret visual you could use to welcome your mate home tonight.

Lois and Curt were sitting at supper one night. Both had busy days at work, and neither was feeling talkative.

When Lois put a piece of chocolate cake in front of each place, she sat down and picked up her fork. Silence continued. As she ate with her right hand, she began to tap on the table with her left hand. She created a pattern of five taps by rolling one finger after another followed by the thumb.

Curt finally spoke. "You are driving me crazy with that tapping!"

Thinking for a minute, Lois said, "Crazy?"

"Yes, can you please stop?"

"Okay, but don't you get the message?" Lois asked.

"What message?" Curt asked.

"Cra-zy a-bout you, cra-zy a-bout you. Hear it? Each syllable is a tap."

Curt's face slowly broke into a grin. His own fingers began to tap a series of four taps.

"What does that mean?" Lois asked.

"I love my wife, I love my wife, I love my wife," said Curt.

Thus began a secret code for that couple. Often when they went out to dinner with friends, Lois or Curt would tap silently on the table, making just enough movement with the fingers for the other to notice. If the opportunity arose, Lois would tap on Curt's leg under the table.

LOVE NOTE HINT: Secret messages can often break the silence after a busy day and set the stage for a romantic evening.

Guests at Caleb and April's wedding reception walked around, curiously looking at the flower arrangements. Some even looked questioningly at their food.

Caleb had always been fascinated with bugs and other creatures. His fascination grew with him into adulthood. At the time of his wedding, his pets included a tarantula and a scorpion.

When he married April, a delightful girl who loved him very much, she took his special interest into consideration when making wedding plans. She requested that the wedding decorator include authentic looking bugs on the flower arrangements at the reception. However, the deepest demonstration of her love came when she was willing to take a taste of the chocolate-covered scorpions Caleb had prepared for the guests!

Acts of Service

I am not a coffee drinker, but when I began to talk with friends about love noting, the paperless love note most appreciated by husbands and wives alike had to do with coffee. Fixing coffee or bringing it to your spouse was top of the list.

Diane's husband doesn't deliver the coffee, but he prepares it. Every morning when she gets up, she finds fresh coffee in the coffeemaker, and beside it, a coffee cup turned upside down with a spoon balanced on top of it. She says the coffee is made because "he knows I greet life with eyelids at half-mast in the morning."

Wendy's husband doesn't even wait for morning. She says, "Almost every evening as I'm working in my studio, he'll come in with a steaming cup of freshly brewed coffee" (a definite love note in Wendy's book).

One day, Merry came into the kitchen to get a cup of coffee and saw her husband, Dave, busily rearranging all the cereal boxes.

"What are you doing?" she exclaimed, amused that such a trivial task could entertain him. Merry had put away those same boxes just that afternoon when she came home from the grocery store.

"You do this on purpose, don't you?" he said with a sparkle in his eyes.

Merry had no idea what he was talking about. Apparently, for the first seven years of their marriage, Dave believed Merry had put the cereal away upside down and backwards just to get his goat! That was not the case. Merry had never really thought about there being a right way and a wrong way to put the cereal boxes on the shelf. Unbeknownst to Merry, her husband had for those same seven years quietly rearranged cereal boxes right side up with labels facing out as his personal labor of love for her.

"Is this just a pet peeve you have?" Merry asked, still laughing.

"Nope," he said. "Since you often make our breakfast, I figured I could pitch in and make the viewing easier, so you can read the boxes and know what you have."

His words triggered an epiphany for Merry: that's the way Dave shows love.

Merry says, "I didn't know when I married Dave he was a cereal-stacking, sandwich-making, what-can-I-do-for-you kind of lover. I'm in awe of my husband's ability to reach out to me on such a practical level."

Dave really knew how to write those love notes! (You can learn more about Dave and Merry's way of love noting at http://www.hopeismyanchor.com.)

LOVE NOTE HINT: Does your spouse eat cereal in the mornings or for snacks? Write a brief love note, and put it down in the cereal inside the wax paper bag. If the box has never been opened, carefully slit a small hole on the small side of the bag, deposit your note, and tape with clear tape. Your tampering will never be noticed when your hungry man goes to open the cereal, and he will be impressed with your creative mailbox!

Dennis Swanberg, internationally known comedian, shares some of his love notes to his wife, Lauree.

"Lauree loves it when I discover on my own something I can do around the house. I make it a habit of looking for burned-out light bulbs and replacing them with new ones. That turns her on!" says Dennis.

Dennis also likes to vacuum.

"Pulling out that central vac hose and vacuuming the house, even if I don't do it that well, makes Lauree happy. It's the effort that says, 'I love you.' I do it even though I know she might come by any minute and say, 'Well, if you are going to do it, at least do it right!'"

Filling a gap for your spouse is also a love note.

Elaine is short. She has been married to Carl for over twenty years. She says, "Carl seems to be flattered when

I ask him to reach things on high shelves. He loves to make things easier for me in the kitchen. If there is ever a new gadget on the market, he wants me to get it to save time for me."

Carl also likes to fix things around the house. He keeps things in good repair and nails up pictures, builds shelves, and oils squeaky door hinges.

Tasks like that may seem very mundane and unimportant, but if you couldn't reach a light bulb to change it or couldn't take a shower in your bathroom because the drain is stopped up, you would really appreciate Carl's type of love notes of service.

Pillow Talk

I am so glad God made us to help each other. I'm short, and you are tall. I like to cook, and you like to clean up. I thank God for my fix-it man!

Jennifer and Brad are bad about leaving their shoes in the middle of the floor, although she will admit she is worse than he.

Brad used to ask Jennifer, "Do you know how many pairs of your shoes I just put away?"

"Well," says Jennifer, "he's caught the habit from me now rather than the other way around."

Jennifer and Brad began to argue about putting shoes away: Why couldn't she put his away? Why can't he help her keep things out of the floor? Jennifer says, "My feeling was always, 'I pick up after three kids and myself. Why can't he put his own shoes away?'"

Eventually, Jennifer came to realize that Brad sees her taking care of everyone else and, although Brad wouldn't admit it, he feels left out sometimes. Now, if Jennifer sees a pair of Brad's shoes lying around, she picks them up most of the time, and Brad notices. He likes it. It makes him feel special, too.

LOVE NOTE HINT: *Are your shoes in the middle of the floor? Do you leave your dirty socks by the bed? Are yesterday's clothes draped over the bench at the foot of the bed? Tonight put your stuff where it belongs. See how many nights it takes for your husband to notice and appreciate.*

Martin's business requires that he travel a lot, often overseas. He sometimes leaves written notes under Amy's pillow. However, if you ask Amy what love note she likes the best, she does not choose the written ones.

"It's the bubble baths," says Amy. "Martin really shows he loves me when he runs a bubble bath for me and puts the boys to bed. When he does that, I feel so pampered and loved."

Pillow Talk

Every bubble tells me you love me. Thank you for helping me relax.

Judy loves roses. For years her husband, Trent, bought them from the florist. One day when they were visiting a friend, Trent noticed that outside the back door was a beautiful rose garden.

"How hard is it to grow roses?" asked Trent. "Do they take a lot of special care and attention?"

"Not really," his friend Jane replied. "You do have to take care of them, but it's not hard."

An idea was already stirring in Trent's mind. Judy has always loved roses. Every time they visited friends who had gardens, she really "oohed" and "aahed" over them. He decided he could plant a rose garden in their yard. The next weekend, Trent began his work.

Judy was so excited over Trent's idea. "He decided to create this rose garden just because I love roses. He doesn't particularly like to work in the yard, but because I love roses, he has done it. What a love note!" Judy says.

My husband has never planted a rose garden. But at his place of work, a rose garden covers an entire bank at the entrance to the building. The caretaker takes pleasure in growing them and loves to share. Those who work in the building have carte blanche to pick roses—so John does.

Occasionally, John will come home with one beautiful long-stemmed rose for me. I always love that. It doesn't matter that it didn't cost as much as a bouquet from the florist. He thought of me enough to go climb the bank to cut one perfect rose. A great love note!

LOVE NOTE HINT: *Flowers don't have to be bought from the florist. If you don't have a green thumb, make friends with a neighbor who loves to grow flowers, and, with permission, stop by his garden and pick one on the way home at night.*

Wendy wanted to do something to surprise her husband. Her days had been so full of responsibilities with their two young children that she hadn't had much time lately for him.

What could I do? She thought.

Knowing that Tim really liked to have a clean car, she picked that for the surprise. She put on her swimsuit, went outside, and washed the car. She also vacuumed, threw away trash, and scrubbed the tires.

When Tim discovered Wendy's love note of service, he was surprised, since washing the car had always been his job. He was genuinely pleased at her efforts.

Wendy got a surprise out of it, too—Tim's response. She expected Tim to be excited about his clean car, but she didn't expect him to talk about it for days, constantly reminding her what a nice thing she had done for him.

That was several years ago. Now, Wendy is the regular car washer.

"I learned that was something I could do for Tim that was an act of love. I continue to wash and clean out the car once a week. Now whenever we go on trips, the car is clean and ready to go. Washing the car that day years ago has paid tremendous dividends in our relationship."

Washing the car is definitely an appreciated love note, but the car can also be involved with other types of love notes. For instance, one of Cecil's love notes to Virginia, his wife, required him to get in the car and go.

Virginia taught Sunday school for many years. Her little class of five-year-olds always came through the door ready to play with Miss Virginia. If she had any preparation to do, she had to do it before the children arrived.

Most Sundays, Cecil went to the church early and arranged her room for Sunday school. He took all her materials into the room, put out the little chairs, and even vacuumed if he thought the room needed it.

The children never knew that Mr. Cecil's love note to Miss Virginia made a huge difference in their morning.

LOVE NOTE HINT: *Helping your spouse in a regular activity may not be what you consider a love note, but when your action makes your spouse's work easier, it is a definite love note.*

Many acts of service can be considered love notes. Here are a few:

♥ Folding clothes when you notice the dryer has turned off.

♥ Keeping the grass mowed. We all like to turn in the driveway and see a well-manicured lawn. At our house, the lawn does not have to be evenly trimmed with every blade of grass in place; just keeping the grass short enough so the snakes can't hide in it is a much appreciated love note!

♥ Noticing when your mate is almost out of deodorant and toothpaste and making sure he has refills on hand.

♥ Keeping the gas tank full of gas. My grandfather always said that if the tank was only half full, it was time to go to the gas station, and he diligently kept my grandmother's car full of gas.

Kitchen Love Notes

A great kitchen love note comes to me from my husband daily a few minutes after five o'clock. Almost without fail the phone will ring.

"Hello."

"Hi, dear, how was your day?" John asks. "Did you get a lot of writing done?"

"Oh, it's been pretty good," I reply.

"Am I cookin' tonight?" he asks.

"I'm afraid so. I haven't been away from the computer much today."

"Well, then, where would you like me to stop on the way home?"

This conversation is our norm just about every week-day. It's not that I don't know how to cook or couldn't figure it out, but as a love note to me, John has freed me from that responsibility . . . at least during the times I am working on a project.

Occasionally when he asks the standard question, I reply, "No, it's my turn to cook tonight. I have already cooked supper, so come on home and enjoy it."

The wonderful thing is that it doesn't really matter who cooks. It is such a blessing to be able to eat dinner together.

LOVE NOTE HINT: Could you cook a meal for your spouse today? Maybe you could do some other chore that is normally his or hers to do. It may be a special blessing to be freed from a routine chore for a day or two.

Rich is an outdoorsman. He loves to fish, hike, and go mountaineering. Recently when he returned from mountaineering, Lissa made for him his favorite meal of grilled wild salmon and flourless chocolate cake.

My husband, John, also loves to fish. I grew up in a family of fishermen. I had never cooked a fish before our wedding, but I had watched enough fish being cooked to think I could do it. I always wondered why my dad cooked the fish on the porch outdoors. After I had my first newlywed fish fry and enjoyed the aroma in the house for a few days afterward, I understood why!

John has also discovered he enjoys hunting. I knew what a dove was, but had never cooked one. The first time he brought home his limit, twelve birds, our family was so excited. The girls weren't so sure they wanted to try it, but my son thought eating doves you had gone to the field and shot yourself was a cool thing.

John and my son, Jeff, spent a long time in the carport cleaning our prize supper. When they finally appeared in the kitchen, they both were spattered with blood and had feathers stuck in their hair. They proudly held out a plastic container.

"Look," they said. "Supper."

I looked in their little bowl and saw the skinned dove breasts. The quantity appeared to be enough for hors d'oeuvres for one and a half persons.

"Wow," I said, "those are nice."

The boys beamed.

Taking the container, I washed the little bird breasts and began to wrap them with bacon. I wrapped one piece around and then another; surely an extra piece of bacon would make them go further. Following the instructions of another hunting friend, I put them in the oven to bake while I readied the rest of the meal.

At suppertime, the family appeared, hungry after all their work. On the table were two bowls of steaming veggies, a big bowl of salad, and a large platter with twelve bite-size dove breasts.

Wanting to maintain the family's excitement, I passed the dove to the children. The girls were not overly enthusiastic. "Help yourself," I said.

Before the platter was around the table, the first diner had taken a bite. "Wow! These are really good. Save me another one."

We quickly learned that since there is a limit on how many doves you can kill in one day, there would have to be a limit on how many dove breasts each person could eat!

A few years later, my husband's growing interest in hunting led him to try deer hunting. Shooting at Bambi? I wasn't so sure about that.

One day the dreaded telephone call came.

"Guess where I am?"

"Out in the field, enjoying nature?"

"No," he said proudly, "on the way to the abattoir."

The abba-what?

"I'm going to get my deer processed. I just shot one." The excitement in his voice was unmistakable.

"Great. What do you do with a processed deer?"

"Cook it. We are going to have meat for the winter!"

I had not heard of someone worrying about meat for the winter since I read the story of the Pilgrims landing the Mayflower! Were we going to have to invite the Indians to the feast?

I didn't tell him of my misgivings about cooking deer, though. While he was on his pilgrimage to the abattoir with his prized deer, I got out the cookbooks. If he was going to shoot it and have it processed, I guess I was going to have to cook it.

I quickly learned several things about deer hunting and cooking:

♥ If he kills it, you must cook it!

♥ If you cook it, you must not tell anyone what you are cooking.

♥ If you serve deer, you must make sure the finished product doesn't taste like deer!

Pillow Talk

I am so proud of my hunter.
I don't ever have to worry about our
family going hungry, because you can
always go out and hunt for a meal!

107

Ginger has always been a tea drinker, and her husband, Scott, has recently become more of one (trying to cut down on sodas). However, he doesn't care for flavored teas, which Ginger loves. So Ginger's love note to Scott is to purchase regular boring old tea for him and keep a pitcher of it in the refrigerator. Scott's love note to her is to buy the sugar-free flavored syrup to put in her tea. When she pours the syrup in the tea and enjoys drinking it, she is reminded that Scott was thinking of her.

"It's a little 'love ya' pick-me-up," Ginger says.

Every summer during the family beach vacation, Jim makes breakfast one morning for the whole gang. His specialty is "birds on a nest" (an egg fried in the center of a piece of toast). Jim has been making this breakfast treat for many years, including premarital years.

Jim's standard in cooking the eggs is to maintain a runny middle. His wife cringes at the sight of runny egg yokes; so after getting married, Jim adjusted his cooking style to accommodate his wife's fried egg preference. She gets her bird on a nest with a well-done middle.

"I make piles of birds on a nest," Jim says, "and no matter how many people I cook for, my wife gets hers the way she loves them."

Brand Name Love Notes

"Chris and I use the stickers off of bananas (you know the little round ones that have the brand name on them)," says Tracey. "We put them on each other's things to show that we're thinking of each other."

"For instance, when I changed cell phone companies, I told Chris that I did not want to get rid of my cell phone because of the worn Del Monte sticker on the back of it. It had been there for more than two years, and every time I saw it, it made me smile. I knew Chris had put it there one time when he was thinking of me."

The next morning, Tracey was very surprised to find another sticker on the back of her brand-new cell phone. "It made it much easier to part with the old one!" she said.

Pillow Talk

I'm stuck on you!

Whenever Scott sees a box of snack cakes in the house, he grabs the scissors and carefully cuts the picture of Little Debbie off the box. His wife, Deb, will find the picture taped to the bathroom mirror. Underneath the picture of Little Debbie, he writes various messages, using the picture as the first two words: "Little Debbie has the best kisses" or "Little Debbie has the best treats."

It is always a treat for Deb to get up in the morning and find one of Scott's notes.

Louise, on the other hand, does not receive snack cake blessings from her husband, but other foods provide opportunity for him to share a love note. Louise has severe temporomandibular joint (TMJ) disorder, and it is difficult for her to eat hard foods. When they go out for a burger and fries, Louise's husband just reaches over and eats the extra crispy fries off her plate, leaving the soft ones for her. He eats her pizza crust, too!

How is that a love note—eating Louise's hard food? It lets her know that her husband is aware of her problem and wants to help her avoid situations that cause discomfort or pain.

Unexpected Gifts

When Candy was a little girl, she spent many days with Mammy, her grandmother. Mammy was a great home-maker and taught Candy much about cooking, sewing, and gardening. The thing Candy remembers most about her grandmother is the way she smelled. Mammy used Rose Milk lotion every day, so she smelled of roses. Her house also smelled of roses because she grew them in her garden and kept some in her house.

One day Candy discovered that Victoria's Secret had wonderful rose lotion that reminded her of Mammy. For several years, Candy, too, smelled like roses with the help of this lotion.

Victoria's Secret eventually discontinued the lotion, much to Candy's dismay. At a semiannual sale, the remaining warehouse stock of the rose lotion was made available. Candy didn't know about the sale, but her husband did. He just happened to be walking in the mall and saw the sale. Jim bought for Candy every bottle they had.

Candy says, "I used the lotion for two years and felt like I was wrapping myself in a hug each time."

LOVE NOTE HINT: We don't always realize the importance of smell in our lives. All of our senses contribute to our sense of belonging and feeling loved. Is there a special smell or fragrance that would take your husband or wife down memory lane? Recreate that pleasant smell today.

For a gag wedding gift, someone gave Bo and Hannah an interesting plaque. It was a little boy holding a pink pig. The little boy had a mischievous look on his face. Someone said it reminded him of Bo. After the couple graciously thanked the giver, the boy and his pink pig took up residence in the hall closet.

One day several years after they were married, Bo had to be gone a few days on a business trip. Hannah was looking for a very special way to say, "Welcome home." When taking her coat out of the closet, she spotted the plaque. *Perfect,* she thought.

Hannah took the plaque down from its comfortable resting place, carried it into the kitchen, got a damp rag, and dusted it off.

"Welcome home," she wrote on a piece of cardboard. "We missed you."

She taped the cardboard to the plaque in a way that made it look as though it was attached to the ribbon around the pig's neck.

Now where shall I put it, she thought. She carried it around the house for a few minutes looking for that perfect spot. Finally, stopping in front of Bo's recliner, she situated the boy with the pig in the corner of the recliner. Bo wouldn't see it right away when he came into the room, but he would see it once he went over to sit in his chair.

That evening when Bo came home, Hannah greeted him with a kiss and told him how much she had missed him. She filled him in on a few things that happened while he was gone and then excused herself to go finish dinner. Bo moved on toward the family room.

Hannah peeked around the corner just as Bo discovered the boy and the pig. "Whaaaaa... Where did you find this ugly thing?"

Hannah couldn't contain her giggles. They both had a great laugh and felt like they immediately connected again despite Bo's recent absence.

Several weeks later, Hannah was getting ready to go out and needed her black shoes. She stooped down to pull them out of their box, and sitting on the box was the boy and pig plaque!

Thus began a merry exchange of the boy and pig. For years, Bo and Hannah worked hard to outdo each other in the hiding of this now famous wedding gift. It has become one of the most memorable gifts they ever received.

Before they were married, Dawn and her husband, Donny, loved to go on dates to the mall. Window-shopping was fun and provided plenty of time for dreaming.

One day, Dawn pointed to a display poster for a perfume company. It was a black-and-white head shot of a man and woman facing each other (positioned very closely, on the verge of a kiss).

"I have two similar wall hangings at home," she said. "That one would fit my collection perfectly."

The next two days, Dawn was out of town. When she returned home, she found a surprise on her bed waiting for her.

The day after their window-shopping discovery, Donny had gone back to the store to try to purchase that display poster. He found the manager, explained the situation, and asked, "Could I just buy that poster, please?"

The manager thought that was such a nice gesture that he gave Donny a poster. Donny placed it on Dawn's bed as a returning home surprise.

Dawn says, "That was a huge love note in our relationship. More of a love 'letter' than note! Without words, he showed that he cared enough to listen to me, to be willing to go to extra trouble for me, and to potentially embarrass himself for me (both the store employees and my mom thought he was a bit odd) . . . all to make me happy."

Thirteen years later, that poster is framed and hanging in Dawn and Donny's room.

Pillow Talk

I think we have a poster relationship.

When Jenn and Jon were first married, extra money was limited, but they were very happy. They pooled their resources and decorated their little apartment together. They loved it!

Jenn loved to cook. One thing that was missing from her kitchen, which she thought she desperately needed, was a spoon rest. It was not in the budget, though.

Their first Valentine's Day as a married couple, Jon bought for Jenn a spoon rest that cost $13, an extravagant gift at the time. It was a perfect gift for a young bride who loved to cook.

Jenn never forgot that Valentine's Day; the spoon rest became a family treasure. Jenn says, "I thought it was so romantic that Jon had listened to me and responded. Now, 13 years later, I still have that spoon rest on the stovetop. I do have another one, and I could now afford to buy six more, but I don't really want to. Just last week, my husband and I were standing in the kitchen, and he said, 'I love that you keep that spoon rest out, even though it's beat up and you don't have to.'"

Love Note Hint: Can you think of a special gift your spouse gave you years ago that could be "recycled" to remind him how much you appreciate his gifting love notes?

Royce doesn't write love notes, but he leaves little thoughtful gifts for Linda on her pillow. One day he found a large soft towel that he thought would be perfect for her to use with her lounge chair. Now every time Linda sits by the pool in her lounge chair, she feels wrapped in love from her husband.

$\mathscr{P}$atience

Jim and Nan had been married only a short time. They were working hard at blending their two families. Nan's youngest son, Donnie, needed to learn how to tie his shoes. Donnie, having a learning disorder, became highly frustrated while trying to learn this task.

"I can't do it," he wailed.

Nan didn't know what to say. She had tried to teach him; every afternoon they worked on it. She was on the verge of agreeing with Donnie. She wasn't sure he could learn to do it.

One day Jim sat down with Donnie and patiently showed him how to tie his shoes. Many days later, Donnie managed to make a very lopsided bow, but he did it!

To Nan, Jim's effort was a tremendous love note because she couldn't muster the persistence and patience that teaching task required, but Jim did.

Pillow Talk

Thank you for loving my children as your own. I am so glad God blended our family.

$\mathscr{R}$ituals

At Doug and Sara's house, it sounds somewhat like *The Waltons* every night.

"Good night, Doug."

"Good night, Sara."

"Sleep tight."

"Sleep tight."

Doug and Sara have been married 19 years. Almost every night during that time, they have made sure they told each other to "sleep tight" before bed.

The first time they had to sleep separately, they were chaperoning a church retreat. Doug sent one of the young persons into Sara's room to tell her to "sleep tight." Even when they are apart, they usually manage to get their bedtime messages to one another.

LOVE NOTE HINT: *Start a good night ritual, and practice it every night!*

Special Praise and Consideration

Nothing says *I love you* louder than praise spoken in front of others. Look for times to praise your spouse in front of other people: his co-workers, your families, the neighbors, and your friends. Speak highly of him or compliment her every chance you get.

"Let him be the expert at something that you could do just fine," says Lissa. "I know my husband wants to feel like a man, important and valuable. Being excellent at something that serves the family is very important to him. When I provide him that opportunity, it shows him that I love him."

Lissa continues, "My husband is an introvert. He often needs quiet space. When I see the look on his face beginning to strain or if we've had lots of social time, I know he probably needs to have some space. I encourage him to go and take whatever time he needs. For instance, recently I told him not to come home from work until he was ready. I could handle the boys. We would be fine. I told him to go and take care of himself. I'll see you when I see you. That is a love note to him, my being concerned about what his unique personality needs to be healthy."

LOVE NOTE HINT: In every way, through your words and in your attitude, affirm your husband. Tell him you are proud to be his wife. Whisper in his ear when passing, "I am so blessed. You are a treasure to me."

LOVE NOTE HINT: Listen. When your spouse sits down beside you and the opportunity for conversation is there, stop whatever you are doing and listen. Put down the newspaper or book. Turn off the television. Look into your mate's eyes. Giving undivided attention says to your husband or wife, "You are important. I want to talk with you more than anything else."

Chapter Six

Love Notes at Work

Often when our spouses leave for work, we feel that they are off to another world and can't be bothered until they walk back through the door. But sending an occasional love note or surprise won't be considered a bother if it is done tastefully and with respect.

When I am at work, no matter how focused I get on a project, I find thoughts of my husband popping into my head frequently. (Actually, I'd rather think about him than anything else!) Something I am working on will trigger a thought. Sometimes it is just a random thought of how blessed I am. He will never know about these thoughts unless I find a way to let him know I am thinking of him.

Office Equipment

My husband's business requires that he spend a lot of time on the telephone; so I know that a large percentage of the time when I call, I am going to get his answering machine. That's okay. He can listen to a few words from me in the midst of his messages from clients. I feel sure that at times mine is the most exciting message on his machine.

Answering machines are great tools to use for leaving love notes for your spouse during the day. Your call lets him know you really appreciate that he is hard at work providing for you and your family. If he has made a specific accomplishment recently, tell him again how proud you are of him.

If you decide to leave a mushy message on his machine (he will like these every now and then), be sure he doesn't check his messages on speakerphone! You don't want the office to enjoy the message along with him.

Often John and I use the computer to communicate during the day. Even if he is on the telephone with a customer, he is sitting in front of his computer, so sometimes I just bypass the telephone altogether.

If I know it is going to be a particularly hard or tiring day, I often write him a quick email: "Hope things are going better than expected." "I'm praying for your meeting at noon." "Did you close that big deal? You are a big deal to me!"

His secretary's husband also knows the value of a love note.

One day, John asked Sandy if she wanted a coffee refill, since he was on the way to the coffee pot.

"Sure," she said. "That would be great!"

John picked up her cup and started around the corner. At first glance, he thought he had picked up the wrong cup—there was writing all over the side of it.

When he looked closer, he read encouraging words from Sandy's husband, Don.

"I love you, Don," the note concluded.

When he returned with her coffee, John told Sandy about thinking he had picked up the wrong cup.

She laughed. "Don never has a pencil and paper with him. He often goes and gets me a cup of coffee before work, so he uses what he has to wish me a good day and to tell me he loves me."

LOVE NOTE HINT: Find something unusual on which to write your spouse a love note: write one on his cup of coffee or place a note inside a folder in his briefcase. Go to his office and write notes on future dates in his calendar. If he is getting ready to go work on his car, beat him to the engine and have a note waiting when he opens the hood! Hide one above the visor inside the car; who knows when he will find that one.

Instant Love Noting

Computers provide tremendous communication opportunities for those of us who spend a lot of time on them at our jobs.

Dena and her husband both work at home. They work in separate offices and on different computers. Often, one will be deep in thought at the computer when a love note pops up in an instant message from the spouse.

"It's fun to get a message from each other once in a while," says Dena.

Lynnette and Jack feel the same way. They, too, both work on computers, often at the same time.

"If we're online at the same time," husband Jack says, "I'll send her a few XOOXXOOXOXOXXO's!"

Computer kisses? Well, why not!

Mart and LeAnne are newlyweds. Even before they were married, they found the computer a great way to communicate while he was at the office and she was working at home.

"We have found that there are things we can say on email that we wouldn't think to say out loud to each other," LeAnne says. "Although they aren't on scented paper, these emails are love notes for us. I have kept every single one of them in a special 'Mart' folder and will print them off someday to keep and to savor as the years go by."

LOVE NOTE HINT: *Computers are great to use for love noting, but don't forget about Uncle Sam. Occasionally write your spouse a love letter, and mail it to work. Use fancy stationery, spray it with your perfume, and pour your heart out. Tell your spouse some of the wonderful things that you love about him.*

Ginger and Scott call each other every day at 10:00 A.M. just to say, "I'm thinking about you, and I love you."

Ginger says, "When I miss a 10:00 call because of a meeting, Scott will call back and say, "What am I, chopped liver?"

Pillow Talk:

Never thought I'd say it,
but I love chopped liver!

Decorating with Love

Remodeling a house also provides opportunities for writing love notes to each other. When Kristi and Jim bought their first house, it was a fixer-upper. In fact, almost everything had to be torn out and replaced: walls, floors, etc. Once the new materials were in place, they had to be primed and painted. In the kitchen, they decided to put new tile in place of the old.

One evening, Kristi was pulling up old tiles as Jim painted kitchen cabinets.

"I noticed she was not making the constant scraping noise any more," Jim relates.

"Finished?" he asked.

"Not yet," she said.

She was trying to write Jim a note while he was working in the other room. *He'll find it when we start laying the new tile,* she thought.

As they primed and painted, they put little love notes to each other on the material that was to be covered, a testimony to their love that would be with the house forever.

To include the element of surprise, Kristi and Jim tried to leave their notes without the other seeing them. That way they would be found in the morning. Each day brought forth a new hunt for treasures of affection.

Pillow Talk

Kristi was here. This note will be here forever. Kristi loves Jim forever, too . . . even longer than this note will be here! (These love notes will be hidden under the new sheet rock and tile of their remodeled home.)

Our homes and offices speak volumes. Many times the best way to learn things about someone you don't know very well is to observe their chosen surroundings.

Recently I visited the office of the president of a large corporation. The furniture was plush and the décor classy. Framed pictures adorned the walls and the bookcase. I admired them all: pictures of him with famous people and signing big deals, lots of expensive artwork, and a less obvious, small picture. As I observed the small picture of a beautiful lady, he said, "That's my wife." It was notably the smallest picture in his collection. I don't know what message this sent about his relationship with his wife, but there was a definite contrast in the importance and size of the business pictures versus the family ones.

Several days later, I visited the office of another corporate executive. Her office was tastefully decorated. Beautiful art was displayed on the walls in prominent places, but surrounding her orderly desk were pictures of her family: her husband, each of her children, her family portrait, including the dog, and a big picture of her husband and her in an embrace. The warmth of her family surrounded her, even in her working environment.

Make sure your spouse has current pictures of you and your family. If he needs some new ones, have new ones made and framed. Then on a day when he is out for a little while, go to his office and place the new pictures around his desk. These "love notes" will remind him of how much he is loved every time he looks at them.

Personally, I don't think you can have enough pictures of those you love around you. With an active family, it is difficult to keep a current picture of your husband and each child, but it is well worth the effort. You never know how many opportunities you will have to show off your family just because of a displayed photograph.

LOVE NOTE HINT: Create a photo love note. Find a favorite picture or take a new one. Write a special caption directly on the photo. This photo love note, framed, would be a great gift for any occasion or just because.

Flowers Say It All

Sending flowers to your husband's workplace occasionally is a great way to get your message delivered with noticeable fanfare. He probably won't be expecting to receive flowers, and his co-workers will get the message along with your hubby! If you want to give special meaning to your floral message, research the meaning of different flowers, and select your floral love note based on a deeper meaning. Here are some meanings for a few flowers:

Aster	Symbol of love
Peony	Happy marriage
Primrose	I can't live without you
Stock	You'll always be beautiful to me
Striped carnation	Wish I could be with you
Zinnia	Lasting affection

More meanings can easily be found by doing an Internet search for flowers and their meanings.

Lissa, speaking of love noting with flowers to her husband, says, "I've sent flowers to his office a couple times, and that blew him away. He said every time he saw those flowers, he knew I proclaimed my love for him. It told everyone in his office he was loved."

LOVE NOTE HINT: If you are going to send flowers, send them on Monday. Then all week, people will pass by your hubby's desk and ask, "What are the flowers for?"

Lauren's husband and son are in business together. Both share the same name as well. One day, Lauren decided to send flowers to her husband.

When the flowers arrived at the store, her husband saw the name on the card, but just assumed the multicolored bouquet was for his son. Imagine his surprise to find out they were for him from Lauren. That was the first time Lauren had sent her husband flowers, but it won't be the last!

LOVE NOTE HINT: *If you don't think your guy will be excited about flowers, send a bouquet of balloons instead. A variation on that thought would be to fill his car with balloons while he is at work. For an extra special touch, put a note inside each balloon, or take a permanent marker and write a love note on the outside of each balloon.*

Often things happen during the day, before work, or even before my husband gets up that trigger a fun thing to do later on.

Craig and Lucie also enjoy some fun exchanges, even though they don't usually see each other until very late in the evening.

Craig left for work one morning before Lucie got up. When she went into the kitchen to get her coffee, she found a note from Craig telling her she snored so loudly the night before that he could hear the corn from the neighbor's field pinging off the side of the house. When she went to bed that night, there was an ear of corn in the middle of her comforter!

No pillow talk was necessary that night. The corn said it all!

Chapter Seven

Love Notes Touch Others

Even though you may not realize it and never intend for it to happen, the notes and other expressions of love you leave for your spouse are observed by others. Those who witness your love noting will also be blessed and benefit from seeing kindness and thoughtfulness modeled before their eyes.

Although we didn't realize it for a long time, every time we wrote a note, we were training our children to be thoughtful and encouraging, too. Now that they are adults, I find them writing notes to their spouses, friends, and, yes, parents.

*E*yes of Love

Eight years after she was married to Gene, the love of her life, Jan lost her eyesight. Her unexpected handicap has revealed to the couple new ways to appreciate each other and to show their love for each other. Jan says, "His care for me knows no limit."

Gene often finds himself in unusual situations. When they are in a public place, he sometimes has to put his masculine ego aside. As Gene leads Jan to the ladies' room, he positions himself in front of the door. Many of those who come in after Jan have a puzzled look on their face, but they are met by Gene's sheepish smile. He is committed to an important task.

Gene monitors the time Jan is in the restroom. He can determine with accuracy when she is taking longer than normal, in which case he provides subtle help. Jan says, "He knows I am lost and can't find the exit door. Restrooms have so many doors! He softly taps on the exit door from the outside. That gives me the clue to follow the sound. That way I can find my way out."

When Jan does get lost and finally comes out of the door, she is greeted the same way every time. With a smile in his voice, Gene says, "There's my baby." She reaches out and finds the security of his strong hand as they continue on their way.

Unbeknownst to Jan, those around them smile, their lives having been touched by the love note of one spouse to another.

A Class in Love Noting

Not only do others observe visible love notes or acts of service, they take them to heart. Noticing the efforts of others inspires us to try to be more thoughtful and kind ourselves.

Will and Elizabeth teach a newlywed Sunday school class. If you have been married in the last 25 years and have attended Sunday school at their church, you have probably benefited from their wisdom.

To begin the session each week, Will or Elizabeth usually tells a funny or entertaining story to the class to get things going. The class members were intrigued by all the fun things they have done together and how thoughtful they were of each other.

In the beginning, Will and Elizabeth's stories were just to break the ice. However, they quickly realized that these opening moments of their class were a great teaching opportunity, so they began sharing love notes with these young couples and encouraging them to find ways they could encourage their spouses.

On Sunday mornings, these young couples couldn't wait to get to Sunday school to hear what kind of encouragement Will and Elizabeth had given each other. They particularly liked to hear about how they made Christmas special for each other.

Did Will and Elizabeth's love notes touch others? Many!

LOVE NOTE HINT: *Don't be shy about sharing your love notes with others. You may plant seeds in others' marriages that will grow, blossom, and produce fruit!*

Making Others Wish

Kathy and Bruce faced a challenge when they were first married. Just weeks after their wedding, Bruce took a new job clear across the state of Florida. Kathy not only had a new husband, but was also going to have a new home in a new area of the state.

Bruce had not sold his house yet, so the plan was for Kathy and her daughter to stay behind until it sold. In the meantime, Bruce would share an apartment with a friend who was transferring with the same company. Kathy and Bruce were combining households so they had plenty of items to outfit the apartment.

Kathy lovingly selected items and packed them carefully for Bruce to take with him, inserting little love notes into many of them. She wrote why she thought the particular item would be special to him and remind him of his family waiting to come join him.

Just prior to the move, Bruce's house sold. Therefore, the plan changed, and Kathy and Jennifer were able to quickly pack and move with him. His new company put them up in a long-stay hotel until they could purchase a new home, so Bruce didn't need the apartment after all. They were thankful not to have to endure the time of separation.

However, the weekend before Bruce had planned to move, his friend and intended roommate, Howard, had come and picked up the boxes of items for the apartment. Howard, wanting to relieve Bruce of having to unpack his stuff and wanting to have the apartment in ready-to-use shape, unpacked the boxes and put the things away, not knowing of the change in plans.

Howard says, "I hadn't laughed so hard in years. Every time I opened a box, it was full of Bruce's 'stuff.' Many of the items in the box had silly little notes attached or tucked inside. I know those notes weren't written for me, but I read them anyway."

To this day, when Bruce and Kathy get together with Howard, those notes are a source of many laughs. Yet every time the subject comes up, Howard makes the same comment: "I wish someone cared enough about me to leave me love notes."

LOVE NOTE HINT: *No effort to show love to your husband or wife is ever wasted, and sometimes the impact of it goes further than you ever imagined.*

It's always fun to add a little humor to our love noting. Often pen and paper are not necessary when our "notes" are carefully chosen.

Kathleen's husband works hard every day. His job is in construction, and he often gets very hot. For years, Kathleen has included in his lunch bag an extra towel to be used to wipe away the sweat.

One day, Kathleen felt that her notes in his lunch bag had become pretty routine, so she decided to add a little spice. Before she packed his clean towel that day, she went to her stocking drawer, pulled out one leg of a pair of black stockings (not panty hose), and carefully hid it in the folds of the towel.

Around midday when her husband had gotten really hot, he pulled out his towel to dry off. Out fell the single black stocking.

"Hey, man, what's that?" one co-worker shouted.

"Whoa, where'd that come from?" another asked.

Kathleen's husband took a lot of ribbing from his co-workers that day, but he didn't mind. He grinned with every question. Judging from the fact that they mentioned the stocking for many weeks to come, he realized they were secretly wishing something similar would fall out of their towels. He knew Kathleen had included that stocking as a love note to remind him that life together was fun and full of the unexpected.

Loving Your Spouse's Loved Ones

Some love notes are not particularly fun, but they do speak loudly of our love and sacrifice for our husband or wife.

Marilyn and Thomas go to visit Thomas's mother every Thursday night. They take dinner, help her with odd jobs, and watch one of Thomas's favorite television shows.

Marilyn says, "This little ritual is not my ideal way of spending an evening after I've worked hard all day long. Even though Mother Robinson is a lovely woman, the visit is a draining experience for me. I can't totally relax."

Yet Marilyn has cheerfully participated in this evening for years. She says, "I do this because I love Thomas, and I know he needs to spend time with his mom. Spending this time with her one night each week keeps him from worrying about her and frees him to pay attention to me the rest of the week!"

LOVE NOTE HINT: Is there something you could do for your husband that might take you out of your comfort zone but would definitely be a pleasure to him?

Often other persons in our own families are touched by our kindness to our mates.

When Jim's mother died, he and his entire family gathered for the funeral. Many of the extended family who came from long distances had not met Nan, Jim's wife, or her family.

When he introduced Nan's oldest children (his stepchildren) along with his own, he said, "I want you to meet my children, David, Donnie, Jamie, and Jonathan." He made no distinction between the two sets of children.

"That was a very precious love note to me," said Nan. "It was not only a love note to me, but an affirmation of his love to my children."

LOVE NOTE HINT: Blended families offer unique opportunities for sharing love with each other. When you include your spouse's children or other members of the family as your own, it is a special blessing not only to your husband or wife, but also to those others you have called your own.

*S*weet Experiences

When we moved into our house, my father's housewarm-ing gift was six scuppernong grape plants for our new fence. Not only was he trying to help us cover the fence for privacy, but I think he was also trying to cultivate my husband's interest in gardening. We nurtured and watered those little plants and watched them grow along with our family.

One day the family was gathered under the scuppernong vines, eating the delicious, juicy grapes.

"Mmmm, these are so good."

"I've never tasted anything so sweet."

"How juicy!"

"Why don't you make some jelly?"

I dropped the scuppernong I was enjoying immensely just seconds before. *Jelly? Make it? What was wrong with the stuff you bought at the grocery store?* I realized that this jelly making would turn out to be another love note that involved getting in the kitchen and learning a new skill.

I read a book that explained how to make jelly. The children helped gather the "scuppies" and eagerly began to wash and smash them.

"When I grow up, I'm going to bring my children home every year when the scuppies are ripe!" said our daughter Ginger.

That first year of jelly making was a learning experience for us all. I realized the activity touched my children in a way they would never forget. We quickly learned that making jelly included several ingredients other than fruit juice, sugar, and water.

Extra ingredient #1: Timing. When one member of the family comes in the house and says, "I think it is time," the rest of the family goes to the vine to test the fruit. Even our yellow Labrador liked to get in on this step! Over the years, the children have learned how important timing is. If you pick the fruit too early, it is not as juicy, and the jelly just isn't as good.

Extra ingredient #2: Hard work and sticking to it until the job is completed. Gathering fruit, washing, smashing, cooking, straining, mixing other ingredients, heating lids and bands, boiling the mixture, filling the jars, covering them with the hot lids, washing the pot—all these things must be done. Indeed, this takes a team effort.

Extra ingredient #3: Pleasure. Enjoy the results of a job well done. Dipping toast in the drippings in the pot is just one perk of being part of the jelly-making team. Hearing the *ping, ping, ping* as the lids seal is always cause for applause.

At Christmas, my husband is so proud to be able to share the jelly with his co-workers and friends. The smile on his face tells me that this jelly-making love note has not only touched every one in our family, but will reach far beyond to others as well.

Pillow Talk

Making jelly is a sweet experience.
Being with you is even sweeter.

$\mathcal{P}$assing on the Blessings

Some people like to journal and some don't. Julie was one of the latter.

Early in her marriage, Julie knew she wanted a way to remember some of the special moments with her husband. She found a small cardboard box with a lid and put it in a safe place in her closet. Now when something memorable happens, she jots down a brief note and puts it in her "Blessing Box." When she and her husband want to remember some of the wonderful times they have had, Julie gets that box, and they randomly pull out a few slips of paper to read and enjoy those moments together all over again.

LOVE NOTE HINT: *Create a Blessing Box for your marriage. You may even want to create one for your family, too.*

Do you ever think that you and your spouse may not have enough time together to say all the things you really want to say? Have you ever thought about writing one last love note for your spouse?

This is not a matter of having the last word. This is a matter of leaving a very special legacy for your spouse and no one else.

Choose a tranquil place and an unrushed time. Before you begin to write, spend some time thanking God for the wonderful mate He gave you. Then take all the time you need and write your spouse the longest love letter you have ever written. Reiterate all the sweet and wonderful things that you would want him to treasure. Seal it and store it in a safe place; you could put it in your safety deposit box or you may want to give it to a friend or sister to give to your spouse in the event of your death.

Virginia has done this. "Writing this letter has helped me focus on all the wonderful things about our lives together," she says. "It also helps me live better in the present because I know Samuel [her husband] will have a special message from my heart if anything ever happens to me."

As my sister and I, as well as our families, were blessed by the love noting and scrapbooking our parents practiced, so might your children and grandchildren be blessed when they discover your Blessing Box or detailed love letter.

Chapter Eight

Love Notes on the Go

When your spouse is away from home or works a different schedule than yours, a little extra effort goes a long way. Surprises and notes in the suitcase and briefcase make the absence or distance seem shorter. Frequent notes and calls help him or her to still feel connected with home base and, upon return after an extended absence, make readjustment to home life much easier.

Traveling Surprises

When attending a conference, Margo had just moments to spare before she spoke. Dashing into the bathroom, she grabbed her makeup case and flung it open. In the middle of her makeup was a pin and a red rose, with a note from her husband attached. The note said, "You are beautiful just the way you are. You don't need any makeup at all."

My husband knows that when I attend conferences, snack time is rare. He often calls ahead and arranges for a fruit basket to be in my room for healthy snacking. There is always more than enough fruit to last the entire conference and to help keep my blood sugar stable between meals.

Not too long ago, I arrived at a conference and began to unpack my suitcase. When I took out my pajamas, I found two good-sized plastic bags. Both were filled with trail mix. One had my name on it, and the other had my roommate's name on it.

I wonder why he put our names on them, I thought. I gave Candy, my roommate, her bag and put mine on the bedside table.

That night after several long meetings, we were back in our room. Sitting on our beds, we had a trail mix snack.

"I really like these raisins," Candy said.

Raisins! My wondering was over. I looked at my bag and, sure enough, it had no raisins in it. I don't like raisins.

The reason he put our names on the bags was because John had gone through my bag before he packed it and taken all the raisins out. Being able to enjoy trail mix without having to pick out the raisins is, for me, a definite love note!

LOVE NOTE HINT: Is there some silly little thing you can do for your spouse, like picking the raisins out of the trail mix? That little thing would make a really big impression.

$\mathcal{D}$ifferent Schedules

Kevin and Hannah haven't been married very long. But they have already learned the value of keeping in touch despite work schedules that leave very little together time.

When they first got married, Kevin was still in school. Hannah was already working full time. Hannah left for her job around seven o'clock in the morning and didn't return home until five. Kevin was in class during the day and then went to his job from five in the afternoon until eleven at night. Kevin and Hannah rarely had time for long talks!

To keep in touch, they began to leave notes for each other. They soon realized these notes were a very special part of their relationship, so they purchased a spiral-bound notebook, their "love note notebook," for the purpose of documenting and preserving these notes. Now they both write in this same special book, which is kept in a certain place, so that each of them can always find it. Kevin and Hannah use a paper clip to mark the next blank page, but they are also able to go back and reread previous notes that chronicle their journey as a couple.

This has been a blessing to them and will probably continue long after their schedules allow more together time!

Lucie and Craig have worked on different shifts for years. They planned it that way, so one parent would always be available for their children. One of the ways they have kept their relationship close and fun is through the notes they write to each other. Somehow even the dog, Salem, and the cat, Crash, got into the act. Here are a couple of the notes they wrote to one another:

> "Please don't leave Blues Clues on any more. We're tired of watching it!"
> —Signed, Crash and Salem
>
> (*Lucie and Craig often left the television on to keep the animals company.*)

> "Salem pulled my tail."
> —Signed, Crash

> "Crash was picking on me."
> —Signed, Salem

$\mathcal{H}$ide and Seek Love Notes

Louise loves to hide notes for her husband. The last time Louise's husband went out of town on a business trip, she hid the love note too well. She put it in a pair of socks, which ended up being a pair he did not wear. One morning after he got home, Louise found the note along with an answer on the kitchen table. His answer to her note said, "You are an expert at hiding things. Even though I am already home, I felt very special when I unrolled my socks and found your sweet note. You made my day!"

Another time, Louise slipped a note in hubby's briefcase just before he headed out the door. "As it turned out, he had to do a presentation as soon as he arrived at his destination—no time to go to the hotel, freshen up, have lunch, etc," says Louise. "He had to go right into the meeting. He opened his briefcase and saw my note. He said it helped him relax, knowing I was praying for him.

Pillow Talk

I am praying for you and thank God you are my husband.

Canella's husband, Britt, often travels on youth ministry trips with our church. For every trip, a theme t-shirt is provided. All the young people as well as all the adults have matching shirts, so when they go out as a group they are easily identifiable.

For the summer mission trip, I go along, too. One of my jobs is to wash shirts for everyone. They work outdoors and get very hot each day. Every person has three shirts, so they will have clean ones to wear while the others are being laundered.

Before we leave town each year, several moms gather to put names in the youth shirts, so we can return the clean ones to the right persons. The church staff is asked to mark their own shirts before they leave home.

During one of these trips as I was folding the clean shirts, I looked in the neck of one and saw Britt's name with a very special note right under his name. Britt's wife, Canella, had written, "I'm praying for you."

What a blessing it must be to know that while you are away, your spouse is praying for you every day.

Dena and her husband are often separated because of business. Each occasionally travels for a few days at a time. Knowing they are going to be separated, even for a short period of time, prompts them into action. The person left at home can find notes almost anywhere: the medicine cabinet, drawers, the refrigerator, and, of course, on his pillow. The traveling spouse finds notes rolled up in socks or underwear, in the pocket of the suitcase, in the briefcase, or tucked in the front of the folder holding notes for an important presentation.

Dena says, "Our oldest son is now six. He has joined me in finding ways to surprise Daddy when he is going on a trip. He loves the sneakiness and knowing that his dad will be surprised when he finds each note or surprise."

There are other sly ways to surprise your husband or wife. A wallet is like a little suitcase that your spouse carries everyday. Occasionally put a small note in with the paper money, or use a sticky note to be seen first every time the wallet is opened. Actually, sticky notes are great to stick just about anywhere!

Bruce, who often receives notes and reminders from his wife, Kathy, says, "When I am away from home and find notes that Kathy has hidden for me, I feel really special. I know some men would be embarrassed to admit that they had love notes in their luggage. Not me—my love notes are my prized possessions!"

Bruce sometimes mentions his love notes to his fellow workers. "You know, there is the group who says they would be embarrassed by the notes," he says, "but there is the larger group who seems to turn a little green with envy when I mention my notes."

LOVE NOTE HINT: Find an out-of-the way place to stick a note for your spouse.

Lucie drove to Wisconsin one summer to see her new granddaughter. Craig, her husband, had put a card in her car. "Don't open until you arrive," it said.

When Lucie pulled in the driveway at her daughter's house, she opened the card. It said, "Missing you already."

Lucie felt warmed even before her daughter's warm welcome because of her husband's heartfelt note.

*P*icture Perfect

No matter what type of trip your spouse is on, a touch of home is always welcome. If your husband or wife is going to be away from home for more than a day or two, make a picture postcard to send to him or her at the new destination. Gather the kids and the dog and take a few pictures. Find a few fun locations; be creative. Take a picture of the family eating at Dad's favorite fast food place, and include a message: "Can't wait 'til you're home and can eat with us!" Have the family pose for a portrait, pets and all, and send it to the absent spouse with a message: "Something is missing—U!"

A picture can easily be transferred to a postcard on the computer, or you can just address the picture on its

147

back and add a message and a stamp. Uncle Sam will carry it to its destination. If your spouse is staying in a hotel or is at a facility that has its own mail system, allow an extra day for your card to travel through the system to him or her.

LOVE NOTE HINT: *If you are going to be the one away from home, take time before you leave to address several cards to your spouse. Plan the mailing so he or she will receive one every day you are gone. Ask a neighbor or co-worker to mail them, so you have a better idea of when they should arrive in your home mailbox.*

When James was gone from home on business for several months, Ruth sent him frequent notes. She often included pictures drawn by their children. When Ruth took the children to visit him, they were delighted to walk into his apartment and see all their pictures and notes taped to the kitchen cabinets.

"Being surrounded by pictures from home kept me feeling connected," James said.

"While my husband and I are apart, I keep a journal of what is going on in my mind and heart," says Lissa. "I not only record what I'm doing, but I also write the specific emotions I am feeling about him at that moment. I write what I am specifically missing about him: his heart, his hands, his voice, his eyes, our conversations. I will be even more specific, telling him what I miss about each of those things. Often I include a coupon for a back rub or massage when he gets home."

"If we are going to be apart, I will tuck a note under his pillow or in his suitcase. He draws little pictures for me. So the last time he left to go mountaineering, I drew pictures of all the peaks he was going to attempt to climb and drew him on the summit. He loved that."

LOVE NOTE HINT: *A picture of your spouse accomplishing a goal gives him or her encouragement to keep on toward that goal.*

James and Ruthanne take turns walking Biscuit, the family dog. Biscuit is always glad to go for a walk so he is not selective about who walks him.

One morning James got up very early and decided to see if Biscuit was ready to get up and go. Not wanting Ruthanne to worry, he left her a note. It was not your ordinary note, however. James had drawn a stick man holding a leash to a dog in motion. Translation? Walking the dog!

LOVE NOTE HINT: *Think of a creative way to communicate with your spouse.*

Welcome Home

Sometimes when our spouses travel, we have to pick them up from the airport. If you are picking up your husband from the airport, make his greeting memorable. Dress totally out of character, or wear a trench coat so he or she doesn't know how you are dressed. Wear sunglasses. Hold up a "Welcome Home" sign or a sign with just his name like the hired limousine drivers do. Don't be shy about showing how glad you are to see him; it will be a special blessing to him when your delight in seeing him again is apparent to everyone there.

LOVE NOTE HINT: *Always show your excitement when you and your spouse are reunited, even after short periods of time.*

One January while I was at a conference, a phone call from home brought tremendous disappointment. The first snowfall of the season had arrived without me!

"Don't worry," my husband said, "we have a surprise waiting for you when you get home."

Several days later when I returned home, I was led to the freezer for my surprise. My husband had saved a few snowballs for my return home! They were hard, somewhat misshapen, and not really usable, but to me, they were beautiful. They were love notes that said, "I didn't want you to miss the first snow, so I saved as much as I could. You are special!"

Pillow Talk

It may be cold on the outside, but you always warm my heart.

*E*dible Love Notes to Go

HEALTHY STUFF

Pat claims he can't cook, but every morning when his wife and son leave for school before he leaves for work, he offers them an egg. The ritual goes something like this:

"Hey, Daniel, you wanna egg?"

"No thanks, Dad. I'm good."

"Well, I'll cook you one anyway. You might want it. Somebody will eat it. Hey, Dalene! You wanna egg?"

"No thanks, Sugar. I appreciate it, though. Maybe on Thursday. Once a week is enough."

"Well, I've got one here if you want it. There's a piece of toast, too."

"Thank you. It does look good. Maybe I'll just take it with me and have it for lunch."

And so the story went nearly every single day for the entire school year. Whether they said yes or no didn't matter. Pat was going to cook that egg and send it out the door with them on their 40-minute drive. Sometimes they ate it; sometimes they didn't.

Often the teacher they carpooled with was delighted to get breakfast on the way, so he didn't have to buy it at school. Sometimes the dog got it later that afternoon. One thing was for sure—someone benefited from Pat's consistent efforts.

After all, an egg a day says *I love you always!*

For the last eight or nine years, Susan has had it made—her lunch, that is! Her husband, Joe, has made lunch for her every day. When Susan is ready to go to work in the morning, all she has to do is pick up her lunch from the refrigerator.

Joe is also the breakfast maker at their house. For years, Joe has served her breakfast in bed on Saturday mornings.

For the last several years, due to some health complications for Susan, Joe has made breakfast every day. He is careful to provide a low carb, protein-rich breakfast that will keep her body functioning at its best. During the week, he makes eggs and cheese, and on weekends bacon is added to the menu.

SWEET STUFF

Sometimes it is fun to put a little extra surprise with your notes. Candy manufacturers have made it easy to turn their treats into quick and creative ways to say, "I love you":

Chocolate KISSES and HUGS— "Here's a special kiss/hug for you."

Stick of gum—"I'll stick with you forever."

U-No candy bar—"You know how much I love you? A whole lot more than I can write here!"

Cookie—"You are one smart cookie, but I think I was the smart one when I picked you."

LifeSavers (or a roll of them)—"You are such a lifesaver! Thank you for helping me get the kids to bed early the other night so I could finish my project."

Snickers candy bar—"I snicker when I think of how much fun it will be when you get home."

Symphony candy bar—"Life is a symphony when you are around."

Pack of SweeTARTS—"I am so glad you are my Sweetart!"

Million Dollar Bar—"You are one in a million."

PayDay candy bar—"Thank you for working hard so that you have a regular payday and can provide for us."

Twix candy bar—"Just 'twix you and me, I think you are the best husband in the whole world. In fact, if I lined up all the husbands in the world, I'd still pick you."

Dum-Dum pop—"I'm so proud of your success. You are no dum-dum."

LOVE NOTE HINT: Is there a candy dish sitting around your house? What kind of candy is in it? Next time it is your turn to fill the candy dish, use nuts, M&M's, or jelly beans. When your spouse is not looking, use the candy to spell out a message to him or her on the counter or tabletop.

Many times when I am traveling, I unpack my suitcase to find a tin of homemade butterscotch brownies. My husband rarely cooks, so this is a special treat. He really scores a lot of points with my friends when I pull this delightful treat out of my bag and pass it around.

Here is John's special recipe for butterscotch brownies:

JOHN'S BUTTERSCOTCH BROWNIES

½ cup butter
  (or margarine)
2 cups brown sugar
2 eggs
2 cups flour

2 teaspoons baking
  powder
½ teaspoon salt
1 cup chopped nuts
  (optional)
2 teaspoons vanilla

Melt butter and mix well with sugar. (No need to get out the electric mixer. A big spoon works fine.) Add egg and mix well. Add dry ingredients to mixture and mix well. Add nuts and vanilla.

Spray a 9 x 13 pan with nonstick cooking spray. Spread dough in pan and bake at 350°F for about 30 minutes. Watch closely at the end, and don't overcook. When done, top will be slightly puffed up and not shiny any more. Cut in squares or bars.

My favorite snack to include for John is "Rocks," one of our family favorites. Here's my recipe for Rocks:

ROCKS

2 cups chocolate chips
½ cup peanut butter
1½ cups dry roasted
  peanuts

1 (12.3-ounce) box
  Crispix cereal
confectioners' sugar

Melt chocolate in a large bowl in microwave oven by heating on high for 1 minute. Stir well. Heat 30 seconds more or as needed to melt chocolate. Stir until smooth. (*Chocolate could also be melted in a double boiler over low heat on the stove.*) Add peanut butter and stir until well blended. Add peanuts and cereal and mix until thoroughly coated. A wooden spoon works best for this. Put confectioners' sugar in a plastic bag. Add cereal mixture, close bag tightly, and shake gently until mixture is coated with sugar. If you do a third of the mixture at a time, it is easier to handle. Makes a lot! Store in an airtight container. Enjoy!

LOVE NOTE HINT: Next time you make Rocks, drive to your husband's place of business and leave some in a container with his name on it on his desk or with the receptionist. A favorite snack will be welcome after a long day at work. If it is a hot day, however, don't leave the Rocks in his car, or he would come out to the car and find one boulder instead!

*M*ilitary Love Notes

One year I was traveling with my mother and sister in England. Both Mom and Poo, my sister, are avid collectors and had specific things in mind as we browsed in antique shops and flea markets. I had a small collection of tins at home but was about out of space. I didn't really want to add too much to that collection.

As we looked around, however, it was not the tins that caught my eye. Mom was looking for brooches from the Victorian period, so we often found ourselves at the jewelry counter. As I looked through the sparkling old pieces, it was the Mizpah brooches that intrigued me.

These brooches were made during wartime. Some of them were made in the late 1800s. As I began to study them, I learned they were made from all sort of metals. Many were handcrafted from English sterling silver. Some were made from several different kinds of gold. Still others were brass or some other less expensive metal. They had varied designs as well. One of the most common designs was two hearts side by side joined by a branch of leaves, clover, or forget-me-nots.

Somewhere on each brooch is the word *Mizpah*. It was at a place called Mizpah that Laban said these parting words to Jacob: "The LORD watch between me and thee, when we are absent one from another" (Genesis 31:49 KJV). These words from the King James Version of the Bible are usually inscribed on the brooch.

As soldiers left for war, they gave these brooches to their sweethearts as a prayer and a promise of their friendship and faithfulness. Some of the brooches had a small insignia of the branch of service in which the young man was serving. Others had the Mizpah verse inscribed on one heart and the insignia of the branch of service on the other. The word Mizpah often was written diagonally with the verse inscribed around it. Throughout the time the soldier was gone to war, his sweetheart wore the brooch as a reminder of her loved one fighting in a foreign land.

Do you have a loved one serving our country overseas? If you can't find a Mizpah pin, perhaps you could frame a favorite picture or scripture or laminate it to be kept in the wallet. Touches from home are most welcome, especially when our soldiers are away for long periods.

Another custom that originated many years ago was using the postage stamp to say, "I love you." An upside-down stamp indicated to the recipient that the sender loved him or her. The upside-down position of the stamp for some carried the message "Life is upside down without you!" Most folks look at an upside-down postage stamp and immediately smile, knowing the message from the sender is "I love you."

Pillow Talk

"The Lord watch between me and thee, when we are absent one from another"
(Genesis 31:49 KJV).

Marnie recently spent several years in the armed services overseas. Her husband, Eric, a civilian, was not able to be with her. They wrote letters and were able to talk on the phone occasionally.

Marnie says the lip balm and peppermints were the best things Eric sent to her while she was overseas. The lip balm became a constantly giving love note each day as Marnie applied it to her parched lips. As for the peppermints, "Peppermints were the only thing that would help settle our stomachs in the aircraft on some days," she says. "It was wonderful to have a good supply."

For some of our military personnel serving in Iraq, it has been unusual things that have made the most progress in their relationships with the foreign army.

When Lt. Col. Glenn Bramhall left for Afghanistan, he never thought about the Christmas traditions that he would miss. Lt. Col. Bramhall was commanding 300 troops from all branches of the military. Those troops were there to train and mentor the Afghan national army. This group of Americans was training the Afghans to use tanks and armored fighting vehicles.

As the holidays approached, Bramhall's wife, Faith, and his mother-in-law wondered how they could get some of his favorite Christmas treats to him. Fruitcake was the first thing Lt. Col. Bramhall ate from the Christmas dessert table every year, so Faith and her mother bought two fruitcakes at the grocery store and mailed them to Afghanistan.

When the fruitcakes arrived, Bramhall was excited. He had been working closely with an Afghan general and wanted to share his fruitcake with him.

The general immediately loved this delicacy and demanded to know which bakery had baked it and why was it a secret. "Was it a secret bakery in Kabul?" he asked. He had never seen or tasted anything so delicious. The general enjoyed the fruitcake so much that Bramhall gave him the other fruitcake he had received. Then he called his wife and asked her to send more fruitcake.

By then, it was January and most of the stores had taken Christmas fruitcakes off their shelves. Faith went from store to store in search of more fruitcake.

"There were no fruitcakes anywhere in our town," she said.

A local supermarket manager suggested she contact the Civitan Club. One of their fundraisers was to sell Claxton fruitcakes at Christmas. It just happened that Faith had been the Civinette sponsor at the local high school for several years and knew many Civitan Club members well. She called Sandy Sanders, her liaison with the club.

"I know we had at least one case in the warehouse," he said, "but let me see what I can do."

The first time he called back, he said, "We have at least 24 pounds we could send." Later he called and doubled the amount.

In the end, the local Civitan Club helped to locate and mail to Afghanistan 144 pounds of fruitcake for Lt. Col. Bramhall and his men. Claxton Bakery, Inc., sent another 100 pounds.

"When the fruitcakes arrived," said Lt. Col. Bramhall, "the Afghans were fighting over them. Everybody wanted some."

What started out as a simple love note to her husband serving overseas turned into a real bonding experience for the Afghans and Americans. It was a wonderful gesture of friendship for the Americans to share their Christmas delicacy with those on the other side of the world. Lt. Col. Bramhall emailed the folks at the Claxton Bakery to let them know that their fruitcakes had a big role in the peacekeeping effort in Afghanistan.

LOVE NOTE HINT: *You never know when God is going to use your small efforts to make a difference in a relationship. Listen for His prompting, and don't assume any idea is too simple or too silly to be of value.*

In case you need a fast, easy, and delicious fruitcake recipe, here's what I do.

Purchase a box of quick bread/muffin mix. These are readily available around the holidays. I usually purchase several extras to have throughout the year. Some of the mixes come in flavors, too. I try to get the nut bread mix, as we like lots of nuts in our fruitcakes. Other flavors, such as banana, cranberry, and pumpkin, will work, too.

Prepare one loaf pan by spraying with nonstick spray and dusting lightly with flour.

In a bowl, mix one small container of candied fruit, about a cup of raisins, half cup of pecans or walnuts, and flour. Use just enough flour to coat the fruit and nut mixture. This will help them stay separate and not clump in the batter.

Mix the bread mix according to directions on the box. When mixed well, fold in the fruit mixture. Bake according to directions on box. You will need to check it with a toothpick to make sure it is done. Be sure not to overcook or it will be dry. Once cool, wrap tightly and store, mail, or give to a friend.

If you prefer to make cookies, here's a great fruitcake cookie recipe. John definitely considers it a love note when he, coming through the doorway, smells these.

FRUITCAKE COOKIES

¼ cup butter or margarine
¾ cup brown sugar
1 egg
¼ cup evaporated milk
1 teaspoon lemon juice
1 cup all-purpose flour
¼ teaspoon soda
¼ teaspoon salt
½ teaspoon cinnamon
½ teaspoon cloves
½ teaspoon allspice
dash nutmeg
¾ cup raisins
1 cup chopped mixed candied fruits and peels (*I use the container of mixed candied fruit already chopped*)
1 cup chopped pecans

Cream butter and sugar until fluffy. Beat in egg. Combine milk and lemon juice. Gradually add to creamed mixture. Reserve ¼ cup flour. Sift remaining flour with soda, salt, and spices. Stir into creamed mixture. Mix reserved flour with fruits and pecans. Blend into dough. Drop by teaspoon on lightly greased cookie sheet. Bake at 375°F for 10 to 12 minutes. Makes about 60 cookies.

Before Shana left for her tour of duty, she spent some time in the kitchen. She baked casseroles and put them in the freezer, so her husband wouldn't have to eat out all the time.

Shana knew she would be gone for six months. Before she left she made a set of daily countdown hearts for her husband. This gave him a way to tick off the days until she would be back. Shana bought a package of red construction paper and cut out six months' worth of hearts. On each heart, she wrote something personal: one of her favorite things about her husband, why it was hard to be separated, or what she was looking forward to when she returned home. Every day while Shana was gone, Rodney, her husband, took one heart down from the mirror in the bathroom where she had taped them. Even though Shana has been home for several years, Rodney has saved his heart countdown.

LOVE NOTE HINT: *Counting down to any special event is fun. Try this idea for a birthday, anniversary, or romantic getaway. You can easily make a countdown calendar by purchasing a die-cut note pad. Adjust the number of sheets to fit your event. Write a special message on each sheet, and then tell your husband to tear off one sheet a day. The last day could contain a clue as to something special that would happen at the long-awaited event.*

Chapter Nine

Other Types of Love Notes

Coupons

Who doesn't like to receive a coupon? Whether the coupon is for a service in the community, such as a massage, a free week at the gym, or time off from washing the dishes (available only through a homemade coupon), it's fun to have a little piece of paper that you can trade in for something enjoyable.

Here are some suggestions. Be sure to customize the coupon for your own special someone.

This coupon entitles [spouse's name]
to one afternoon of undivided attention.

This coupon entitles you, [spouse's name],
to a back rub at the time of your choice.

This coupon entitles you, [spouse's name],
to a large bubble bath, drawn and prepared
especially for you. (Companionship in the
bubble bath available upon request!)

This coupon entitles you, [spouse's name],
to an afternoon all to yourself.
Children will be properly cared for and fed.

This coupon entitles you, [spouse's name],
to lunch and a book lover's afternoon.
You will be treated to lunch and unrestricted
time browsing in the bookstore of your choice.
One book purchase is included.

This coupon entitles [spouse's name]
to a walk in the park.
(Hand available to hold.)

This coupon entitles you, [spouse's name],
to one hour of vacuuming/yard assistance.

_____

This coupon entitles you, [spouse's name],
to an afternoon of boating on your favorite lake.
Picnic will be provided.

_____

You could make the coupons the size of business cards. On one side, print "Best Husband in the World"; on the other side, write what the coupon is good for. Be sure to list an expiration date. I have found that if the coupon is good indefinitely, it is much less likely to be used. A year is a good length of time for the life of a coupon.

With the business card coupons, you may want to spread them out, timewise, and hide one a month for your husband to find. Then he will have a surprise to look forward to each month.

Message in a Bottle

We have all watched enough movies to know how romantic it is to discover a floating bottle that contains a special message. In the movies, the scene is usually on the beach, and the lonely man or woman is just casually walking along the beach when the discovery is made.

Take that idea and give it a contemporary twist. Use an empty plastic water or soft drink bottle. Remove the label (If you have trouble removing it, fill the bottle with hot water to soften the glue.), wash the bottle, and allow it to dry.

Write a special message of love to your spouse. Fold or roll the paper so it will fit in the bottle. After inserting the message, recap the bottle tightly.

The next time you fix a bubble bath for your mate, slip the bottle into the tub as a special surprise.

If your spouse does not enjoy bubble baths, think of other options for delivering your message in a bottle. The bottle could be floated in your backyard swimming pool, fountain, birdbath, or fish pond. You could even slip it into his car-washing bucket. If you like to take long walks, you could plan a "finding" by a lake or creek. Prearrange to have the bottle floating in the water; then subtly guide your mate in a walk by the water.

If you and your spouse are going to be apart for a while, create your message in the bottle, and then mail it to him or her.

$\mathcal{L}$ists

Lists are very popular. In fact, one of my husband's favorite books is a book that is made up entirely of lists. It gives lists for everything. So why not put a love note in the form of a list? Consider these ideas:

Top Ten Reasons Why I Love You
    10. You are mine.
     9. You raise one eyebrow when I walk into the room.

8. I have looked at all the other guys around, and you are the cutest.

7. Other guys would leave the room when I guffaw.

6. Life is so much more fun when you are in it.

5. You have cute legs.

4. It's fun to snuggle with you at night.

3. You don't eat onions on your hamburger just because I don't like to smell them.

2. You are a wonderful father.

1. God gave you to me!

Top Five Reasons I Want You for My Valentine

5. You like candy hearts.

4. You send me red carnations.

3. You smooch anytime I want.

2. I feel safe when I hold your hand.

1. As Valentines go, you are the very best.

Top Three Reasons I Like to Go on Vacation with You

3. It's so much fun to do nothing together.

2. You like to eat out, so we have a vacation from cooking, too.

1. You are my best friend.

Top Five Reasons I'm Glad I Married You

5. No one else could take care of me as well as you do.

4. You are such an encourager.

3. I love sitting in front of the fire with you.

2. I see God in you every day.

1. I love you with all my heart.

Top Ten Reasons I Am Crazy About You (specifically from a wife to a husband)

10. You still open car doors for me and walk on the outside of the sidewalk.
9. You remember to put the toilet seat down in the middle of the night almost every time.
8. You call every night and ask, "Am I cooking tonight?"
7. You don't mind when I answer, "Yes," again.
6. You want the grass to always be neat and trimmed.
5. You don't fuss when our checkbook doesn't balance right away.
4. You are my number one cheerleader!
3. You still make my heart race every time I see you.
2. You are as crazy about me as I am about you.
1. I am absolutely sure God made us for each other.

Top Ten Reasons I Am Crazy About You (from a husband to a wife)

10. You never complain about keeping my clothes clean.
9. I come home to a home-cooked meal every night (well, almost every night).
8. You never criticize me in front of the children.
7. You let me think I make important decisions.
6. The house is always warm and inviting.
5. You make me proud when I introduce you to business associates and co-workers.
4. You don't complain about "holding down the fort" when I am away on business trips.

3. You cook English peas because I like them, even though you don't.
2. You make me feel like I am king of our castle.
1. You are a true gift from God.

Codes

When we were children, it was fun to make up special codes to use in letters we wrote to our friends. It was a challenge for them to crack the code. Just because we are older does not mean we have to stop communicating with codes.

Make up a code that is just between you and your spouse. Write him or her a love letter using the code, and let him or her crack the code. One easy code is just to write backwards. Then your spouse can take your message to a mirror and decipher it at once. A tougher code to crack is to write a message omitting all vowels and spaces. The longer the message, the greater the challenge!

Technology Notes

Does your husband or wife carry a cell phone or electronic planner? If so, those items provide more avenues for creative love noting—technological love noting.

When you can borrow the cell phone for a few minutes, put a picture of the two of you together on the screen, so that when the phone is opened, the picture is the first thing seen.

If the phone or planner has a message alarm feature, set the alarm for a time when you know you won't be together, such as in the middle of the work day. Have the reminder programmed to say, when the alarm goes off, simply, "This is a reminder that I love you and hope you have a great day."

Cell phones also allow text messages to travel back and forth between two people. Send a text message every now and then as a special reminder of how much you love your spouse. Unlimited text messaging is very inexpensive and is an effective way to communicate. (If you have teenagers, it is sometimes the only way to get their attention.)

A few people still carry pagers. If your spouse is one of those, take advantage of it. Develop a secret numerical system of messaging one another, so you can leave a message that is understood only by him or her.

Newsletter

These days, computers make it very easy to create your own newsletter. Collect your thoughts and make a "Special Moments Newsletter" or name it the "[Your Last Name] Gazette." Make sure the headlines are all about your mate. For example, you might write an article called "Super Hunk Seen Riding Lawn Mower." The article would be about him riding the lawn mower in the neighborhood and what a nice job he does keeping the lawn manicured. Be sure to include how great it makes you feel to live in a castle where the grounds are always so well kept. Take a picture of him riding the lawn mower to accompany the article.

Include pictures of the two of you doing fun things. Make up a knock-knock joke about your relationship. Add a famous quote or maybe a famous quote from him!

This will surely be a hit with him and anyone else who sees it.

*O*bject Notes

Let ordinary household objects help you send a message to your spouse.

♥ *A puzzle.* When he or she is away, buy a small child's puzzle with 25 to 50 pieces. Open it and remove one piece. Seal it back up and mail it to him along with a note to open when he is finished putting the puzzle together.

Something is missing in my life right now, too—you! Hurry home to me.

♥ *A piece of string with a few knots tied.*

Love is the knot that holds us together.

♥ *An adhesive bandage.*

No matter how bad I feel, you can always make me feel better.

♥ *A rubber band.*

Sometimes life feels like a stretch.
Yet every time we stretch, we grow,
and I love you more than ever.

♥ *A small flashlight.*

You are the light of my life.
I thank God each day for you.

Scripture Notes

The only thing that can give our marriages a solid foundation is to base them on the One who came up with the idea in the first place. God through His Word tells us, "For this reason a man will leave his father and mother and be united to his wife, and they will become one flesh" (Genesis 2:24). God made woman out of man and intended for them to spend their lives together.

Love noting can be a way to enrich that union and strengthen the bond between a man and a woman. God has shown us how to love each other and has instructed us how to draw closer to one another. "I have loved you with an everlasting love; I have drawn you with loving-kindness" (Jeremiah 31:3). Love notes would definitely fall in the category of loving-kindness.

Sometimes we don't feel like very good writers. That's okay. When we can't think of anything to say, we can always turn to the One who has said everything there is to say about love. We have an entire book full of love notes, the Bible. Find a verse of scripture that will bless your mate. Along with the scripture verse, tell him or her how you see that verse being applied in his or her life. Point out ways that you see God using your spouse for His glory.

God's Note: "Look to the LORD and his strength; seek his face always" (1 Chronicles 16:11).

I love your commitment to the Lord.
It is comforting to me to know that you
seek His face in everything you do and
in all decisions regarding our family.

God's Note: "All night long on my bed I looked for the one my heart loves; I looked for him but did not find him. I will get up now and go about the city, through its streets and squares; I will search for the one my heart loves. So I looked for him but did not find him" (Song of Solomon 3:1-2).

I am glad that on your trip you will be gone
for only a few nights. I really miss you.
Your side of the bed seems so empty.
I am thankful that I do not have to go out
and search the streets for you. I know where
you are and that you will be back with us
as soon as your meeting is over. I can't wait.

God's Note: "But seek first his kingdom and his righteousness, and all these things will be given to you as well" (Matthew 6:33).

Seeing you every morning at the table, spending time with God, reminds me daily that you have your priorities in order. Thank you for being such a wonderful example for our children and me.

God's Note: "You will keep in perfect peace him whose mind is steadfast, because he trusts in you" (Isaiah 26:3).

Your trust in God is obvious in everything you do. Having a man of God to share my life with is a true blessing.

God's Note: "Each one should use whatever gift he [she] has received to serve others, faithfully administering God's grace in its various forms" (1 Peter 4:10).

You are so talented, and God has opened doors for you to use your talents doing things for Him. Your heart of a servant makes me love you even more!

God's Note: "Love is patient, love is kind. It does not envy, it does not boast, it is not proud. It is not rude, it is not self-seeking, it is not easily angered, it keeps no record of wrongs. Love does not delight in evil but rejoices with the truth. It always protects, always trusts, always hopes, always perseveres" (1 Corinthians 13:4–7).

Pillow Talk

You are real love to me.

Appendix

A few more tips on how to write special love notes, along with instructions for creating fun and unusual surprises for your spouse, follow:

Acrostic Ideas

Make an acrostic with your spouse's name.

WORDS FOR NAME ACROSTICS

A awesome, amazing, astounding, attractive, adorable, athletic

B brainy, best friend, beautiful, brave, bold, brilliant

C cute, charming, compassionate, courageous, clever, caring

D delightful, dear, dedicated, devoted, darling, daring

E energetic, excellent, efficient, easygoing, enthusiastic, exciting

F fun, funny, friendly, famous, fabulous

G gracious, great, gregarious, genuine, good, gentle

H helpful, healthy, honest, happy, hardworking

I important, insightful, intelligent, interesting, irresistible

J jolly, just, joyful, jovial, jubilant

K kind, keen, kingly, kid

L loving, laughing, lovely, lively, leader

M masculine, moving, muscular, marvelous

N nocturnal, nice, newsy, nifty

O open, obliging, outstanding, original

P pleasant, polite, pure, pleasing, patient, paternal

Q quality, quick, quotable

R right, rare, respectful, royal, responsible

S sociable, sexy, sweet, sunshine, smart, sympathetic

T talkative, tireless, tidy, tender, thoughtful

U unbelievable, upright, unique

V victorious, valuable, virtuous

W wise, warrior, witty, wonderful

X x-cellent, x-citing, x-traordinary

Y young, youthful

Z zany, zestful, zealous

Valentine Extras

Go to the store the day after Valentine's Day, and visit the half-price table. Most likely, you will find hearts of many shapes and sizes, chocolate hearts, love stickers, and other goodies. Stock up. Buy things that can be used as little love notes throughout the year. Pick up a pack of humorous valentines, and sprinkle them in unexpected places every now and then. I found the dollar store to be an especially good source of heart surprises last year. I stocked up on candy hearts, wax lips, big clothespins that had red lips on them, pencils that said, "I love you," and many other things.

Love Prescription

For an easily portable love note system, use an empty pill bottle. Write words or phrases of encouragement on small strips of paper (key word here is *small!*). Roll the strips into a cylinder or fold them individually and place them in the empty pill bottle. Either make a computer label for the pill bottle or write with permanent marker on the outside of the bottle:

> [Spouse's name]
>
> Prescribed by Dr. [Your Name]

Read one note daily. Read and know how much your spouse loves you. On particularly difficult days, dosage may be increased to two!

Fortunate Husband

To give your spouse a fortune he will never forget, personalize a fortune cookie. The next time you eat at a Chinese restaurant, pick up a few extra cookies. Carefully open the outer wrapping. (You need to be able to seal it back together.) Hold the fortune cookie over boiling water with tongs. Once it is soft, pry it open just enough to take out the fortune and insert a fortune you have written especially for your spouse. Steam the cookie a little more, and press it back into the original shape. Allow it to cool, return it to its original wrapper, and seal.

On your next trip to a Chinese restaurant, when your husband isn't looking, replace the fortune cookie he receives with the personal one you prepared for him.

Quotes for Notes

When you don't feel like writing a creative love note, borrow one from someone else! Here are a few suggestions:

What a happy and holy fashion it is that those who love one another should rest on the same pillow.
—Nathaniel Hawthorne

Newlyweds become oldyweds, and oldyweds are the reasons that families work.
—Author Unknown

Love doesn't make the world go 'round. Love is what makes the ride worthwhile.
—Franklin P. Jones

Let the wife make the husband glad to come home, and let him make her sorry to see him leave.
—Martin Luther

Chains do not hold a marriage together. It is threads, hundreds of tiny threads, which sew people together through the years.

—Simone Signoret

People shop for a bathing suit with more care than they do a husband or wife. The rules are the same. Look for something you'll feel comfortable wearing. Allow for room to grow.

—Erma Bombeck

Try praising your wife, even if it does frighten her at first.

—Billy Sunday

Love one another and you will be happy. It's as simple and as difficult as that.

—Michael Leunig

A successful marriage requires falling in love many times, always with the same person.

—Mignon McLaughlin

Souvenir Notes

Make a habit of writing souvenir notes. When you have a big night out on the town, bring home a napkin, matchbook, menu, or other souvenir. The next morning, write on the souvenir a thank you note to your spouse, telling him what a good time you had.

$\mathcal{M}$anly Notes

For husbands, it is easy to come up with frilly little surprises for wives. They can leave trails of rose petals, buy
bottles of perfume, or draw flowers and hearts everywhere. For wives, it is *not* so easy to find things that husbands wouldn't label as too silly; it is hard to find things
that make the statement, "You are a man!" Here are a few
suggestions:

♥ Buy a bag of little green army men. Use them as note
holders. Hide them in his drawers, medicine cabinet or
briefcase. Make sure these notes are macho sounding
rather than drippy and overly romantic.

I'd go to war over you!
Our love is worth fighting for.

♥ Pick up some smooth rocks or pebbles. Scatter them
around the house with notes attached to them. If a rock
surface is large enough, write directly on the rock!

You rock my world. Every time
I see you my heart goes wild.

♥ In the fall, gather a bunch of leaves that have already
changed color and fallen from the trees.

I'd fall for you all over again!

Instead of linking your notes to the object, you may want to do a series of notes that applaud your husband's attributes:

♥ I know *armies* of women would love to have you, but I'm so glad you chose me.
♥ You are my *rock*. I am so thankful for a Christian husband.
♥ I'd *fall* for you all over again because you are the most thoughtful man I know.

Cover the Paper

To make a strong point, get a piece of pretty stationery, and write as many times as you possibly can on that one piece of paper, "I love you." Write horizontally, vertically, diagonally, upside down, and backwards— every which way. Write until the paper is covered and there is not a vacant spot left!

Bathroom Reading

Sneak into the bathroom and unroll the toilet paper. Write your spouse a note several squares into the roll. Then reroll the paper so that he won't see the note when he comes in.

Fan the Flames

If you have a ceiling fan, look for an opportunity to let that help you tell your spouse how special he is. Cut hearts out of construction paper or card stock; make the hearts several colors and sizes. When your spouse is away from the house, place the hearts on the top of the fan blades while the fan is turned off. Make sure no one turns that fan on before he does! He will enjoy his shower of hearts straight from your heart.

Good Places for Notes

Good places to leave love notes are endlessly bountiful, but here are a few:

  On his or her pillow
  In the refrigerator on his favorite beverage
  In a shoe
  Under pajamas
  In the lunch box
  In the shower (protected, of course, in a plastic bag)
  Inside a magazine he or she is reading
  In the briefcase
  On the steering wheel of the car
  Inside the gas tank door on the car
  Taped to the vitamin bottle
  In the coffee mug
  In a folded towel
  In his tool box
  On the lawn mower

Notes in the Margins

Buy a tear-off calendar or a small, quickly read book for your spouse. Before you give it to him or her, read it yourself. Make notes on the pages that particularly remind you of him or her. Comment on why that page triggers a memory. Point out his or her attributes that you appreciate. Your notes will make that gift a personalized surprise.

Pancake Notes

Pancakes are a favorite meal at our house. Pancakes are also a great way to send a message of love to the diner. There are several ways you can do that:

♥ Draw a heart with the pancake batter. This is easily done by first making two small circles side by side and then adding a third underneath. Pull the spoon slightly down as you lift it from the third circle to make the point of the heart.

♥ Tint some of the batter pink with food coloring. With the pink batter, draw a small heart on the griddle. Cover the pink heart with regular batter. When you turn the pancake, you will have a pink heart in the center of the pancake.

♥ Does your husband have a special interest? Does he like to fish? Draw a fish with the batter. Does he like to read? Draw a book. Does he play golf? Draw a golf club. Does he like to hunt? Draw a gun or deer. (For detailed items such as a deer, I just do the best I can; then when serving, I announce the shape of the day!) No special artistic talent is required for this love note; just use your imagination and test your spouse's.

Love Notes

For you to photocopy and personalize.

Top **10** Reasons Why I Love You.

10.

9.

8.

7.

6.

5.

4.

3.

2.

1.

Pillow Talk

Kisses available anytime

Top **3** *Reasons Why I Love You.*

3.

2.

1.

Top **5** *Reasons Why*

_____ .

5.

4.

3.

2.

1.

Love Note

New Hope® Publishers is a division of WMU®,
an international organization that challenges Christian
believers to understand and be radically involved in
God's mission. For more information about WMU,
go to www.wmu.com. More information
about New Hope books may be found at
www.newhopepublishers.com. New Hope books
may be purchased at your local bookstore.